"Tilting at Windmills"

"Tilting at Windmills"

History and Meaning of a Proverbial Allusion to Cervantes' *Don Quixote*

Wolfgang Mieder

"Proverbium"
in cooperation with the
Department of German and Russian

The University of Vermont
Burlington, Vermont
2006

Supplement Series

of

Proverbium
Yearbook of International Proverb Scholarship

Edited by Wolfgang Mieder

Volume 21

Cover Illustration:
Engraving (1844) by Alejandro Blanco from
H.S. Ashbee, *An Iconography of Don Quixote, 1605-1895.*
London: Bibliographical Society, 1895, p. 91.

ISBN 0-9770731-3-0

Manufactured in the United States of America
by Queen City Printers Inc.
Burlington, Vermont

Dedicated
to all my friends in the
Department of Romance Languages
at the
University of Vermont

Contents

Introduction 9

1. Fighting windmills – a polyglot phenomenon 10

2. The adventure of the windmills 11

3. Windmills and proverbial duels 25

4. The proverbial phrase "to have
   windmills in one's head" 28

5. The proverbial phrase "to fight with a
   windmill" 34

6. Variations of the proverbial expression
   "to fight windmills" 43

7. The proverbial phrase "to tilt at windmills" 45

8. The survival of the windmill-episode in
   cartoons and caricatures 64

Notes 89

Appendix 99

Introduction

While most proverbs and proverbial phrases are based on repeatedly observed or experienced natural phenomena or human behavior, there are also numerous formulaic expressions that summarize events from classical mythology, parables of the Bible, Aesop's fables, folk narratives, and also literary works into succinct and memorable statements that belong to the general cultural literacy of humankind.[1] The "Trojan horse," "Achilles' heel," "the labor of Sisyphus," "Pandora's box," "the Gordian knot," "the golden calf," "the handwriting on the wall," "wolves in sheep's clothing," "sour grapes," "the Pied Piper," "a Faustian bargain," and "beauty and the beast" readily come to mind. The proverbial allusions can be heard throughout the world in oral discourse, and they appear with considerable frequency in all types of writing. This is doubtlessly also true for the well-known phrase of "tilting at windmills" that alludes to Don Quixote's unforgettable adventure with the windmills in chapter eight of part one of Miguel de Cervantes Saavedra's massive novel *Don Quixote* (1605/1615). In fact, if people know anything about this voluminous literary work, it is that Don Quixote in his delusions mistakes windmills for giants and consequently loses his human fight against the overpowering machines.[2] One might even go so far as to maintain that the entire novel has basically been reduced to the word "quixotic" in the meaning of being impractically idealistic and the proverbial phrase "to tilt at windmills" with its message of attempting a noble but unrealistic struggle with no chance of success.

1. Fighting windmills - a polyglot phenomenon

In many European languages, and certainly in the major Romance, Germanic, and Slavic languages, the windmill-scene has been abridged to the proverbial phrase "to tilt at windmills" with a number of variants, such as "to fight with windmills" or "to battle against windmills." The windmill-adventure found its way into these different languages as the novel was translated and read by ever more eager readers, and the allusion to it might have quite naturally and independently become proverbial over time. Since the proverbial expression as such does not appear in the novel itself, it might also have entered other languages by way of loan translations from the Spanish "acometer molinos de viento," the French "se battre contre les (des) moulins à vent,"[3] the German "gegen (mit) Windmühlen kämpfen," [4] the Dutch "tegen windmolens vechten,"[5] the Russian "srazhat'sia s vetrianymi mel'nitsami,"[6] and in more modern times by way of global distribution of the English version of "to tilt at windmills." The history of this proverbial allusion in various national languages deserves specific studies, but as an example of the different stages of its international distribution it might be pointed out that the phrase in Hungarian became established only in the first half of the twentieth century,[7] while it was already current in German during the second part of the eighteenth century.[8]

Of special interest in this regard is also that the Spanish version "acometer molinos de viento" and its variants "luchar contra molinos de viento" and "atacar los molinos de viento" have never achieved the popularity that the phrase gained in German or English, for example.[9] In Spanish the phrase is regarded more of a literary allusion to the novel, while in German and English the phrase has achieved a much more general proverbial status, i.e., people do not necessarily always associate it with Cervantes' novel. The proverbial expression has taken on a life of its own, and yet, since especially in the United States the younger generation has no particular relationship to windmills any longer, the phrase might well be in actual decline. While it is still to be found in the print media, American students whom I surveyed have stated for the most part that they hardly know the windmill-phrase (if at all) and that they would not really make use of it in their oral or written communication.

Nevertheless, the verbal allusion to fighting windmills took a very early hold in the English language especially, and unless earlier references should still be found in Spanish, it will be shown that the proverbial expression of "tilting at windmills" and its variants had a definite start in Britain while Cervantes was still working on the second part of his famous novel.

2. The adventure of the windmills

The actual account of the windmill-adventure does not even comprise two of the 940 pages of Edith Grossman's new translation that appeared in 2003! And yet, the following pertinent passages contain in many ways the crux of the novel:

> As they [Don Quixote and Sancho Panza] were talking, they saw thirty or forty of the windmills found in that countryside, and as soon as Don Quixote caught sight of them, he said to his squire:
> "Good fortune is guiding our affairs better than we could have desired, for there you see, friend Sancho Panza, thirty or more enormous giants with whom I intend to do battle and whose lives I intend to take, and with the spoils we shall begin to grow rich, for this is righteous warfare, and it is a great service to God to remove so evil a breed from the face of the earth."
> "What giants?" said Sancho Panza.
> "Those you see over there," replied his master, "with the long arms; sometimes they are almost two leagues long."
> "Look, your grace," Sancho responded, "those things that appear over there aren't giants but windmills, and what looks like their arms are the sails that are turned by the wind and make the grindstone move."
> "It seems clear to me," replied Don Quixote, "that thou art not well versed in the matter of adventures: these are giants, and if thou art afraid, move aside and start to pray whilst I enter with them in fierce and unequal combat."
> And having said this, he spurred his horse, Rocinante, paying no attention to the shouts of his squire, Sancho, who warned him that, beyond any doubt, those things he was about to attack were windmills and not giants. But he was so convinced that they were giants that he did not hear the shouts of his squire [...].

Just then a gust of wind began to blow, and the great sails began to move, and, seeing this, Don Quixote said: "Even if you move more arms than the giant Briareus [a giant from Greek mythology with fifty heads and a hundred arms], you will answer to me." And saying this, and commending himself with all his heart to his lady Dulcinea, asking that she come to his aid at this critical moment, and well-protected by his shield, with his lance in its socket, he charged at Rocinante's full gallop and attacked the first mill he came to; and as he thrust his lance into the sail, the wind moved it with so much force that it broke the lance into pieces and picked up the horse and the knight, who then dropped to the ground and were very badly battered. Sancho Panza hurried to help as fast as his donkey could carry him, and when he reached them he discovered that Don Quixote could not move because he had taken so hard a fall with Rocinante.

"God save me!" said Sancho. "Didn't I tell your grace to watch what you were doing, that these were nothing but windmills, and only somebody whose head was full of them wouldn't know that?"

"Be quiet, Sancho my friend," replied Don Quixote. "Matters of war, more than any others, are subject to continual change; moreover, I think, and therefore it is true, that the same Frestón the Wise who stole my room and my books has turned these giants into windmills in order to deprive me of the glory of defeating them: such is the enmity he feels for me; but in the end, his evil arts will not prevail against the power of my virtuous sword."[10]

This then is, in short, perhaps the most famous of Don Quixote's "misadventurous adventures," [11] as Cervantes calls his hero's knightly exploits that are based on a fascinating "mixture of intelligence and madness."[12] Clearly the windmill-episode follows a structural pattern that can be observed of most of Quixote's adventures, namely: 1. reality is stated in narration; 2. Don Quixote willfully transforms reality; 3. Sancho Panza points out the reality of the situation; 4. Don Quixote rejects Sancho's interpretation; 5. Don Quixote either invokes or commends himself to Dulcinea; 6. Don Quixote undertakes the adventure; 7. Don Quixote, when not victorious, blames his defeat on enchantment.[13] Early in the novel and before the crucial windmill-adventure, Cervantes as the narrator gives his readers a clear idea of what motivates the deranged Don Quixote on his many sallies:

> The truth is that when his mind was completely gone, he had the strangest thought that any lunatic in the world ever had, which was that it seemed reasonable and necessary to him, both for the sake of his honor and as a service to the nation, to become a knight errant and travel the world with his armor and his horse to seek adventures and engage in everything he had read that knights errant engaged in, righting all manner of wrongs and, by seizing the opportunity and placing himself in danger and ending those wrongs, winning eternal renown and everlasting fame.[14]

But what then is the purpose of the windmill-adventure in the greater realm of things, and how can it be considered "as a prototype of Quixotic-insanity,"[15] "emblematic of the entire novel,"[16] or "the paradigmatic Don Quixote adventure?"[17] Phrased differently, the question is what do the windmills symbolize in this bizarre adventure that has inspired scores of visual artists to illustrate the scene and that continues to be mentioned in literature and the mass media in the form of allusions or proverbial phrases to this day? Before attempting an answer to this vexing question, it might be well to take at least a glance at some of the dozens of artistic interpretations of the windmill-scene by illustrators of the novel:

[1640] An engraving by Jacques Lagniet and Hieronymus David in a French edition of the novel, showing Don Quixote with his broken lance falling off his horse while Sancho rushes to assist his master.[18] [Fig. 1]

[1648] An anonymous engraving in a German edition of the novel, depicting Don Quixote glancing in disbelief at his broken lance of which parts are flying through the air with Sancho standing by on his donkey.[19] [Fig. 2]

Figure 1

Figure 2

[1779] A more drastic drawing by Daniel Chodowiecki and engraved by D. Berger in yet another German edition of *Don Quixote*, showing the knight errant and his horse defeated on their backs with Sancho about to dismount his donkey in order to help.[20] [Fig. 3]

[1825/50] Folk art first depicting Don Quixote and Sancho riding along as the inseparable pair, and then again Don Quixote with his horse on the ground, his lance stuck in one of the windmill's sails, and Sancho rushing forward to survey the mishap.[21] [Fig. 4]

[1843] A drawing by the German artist Adolph Schrödter with Don Quixote being hurled through the air, his horse crashing to the ground, and Sancho beside himself with horror.[22] [Fig. 5]

[1844] An engraving by the Spanish artist Alejandro Blanco, showing Don Quixote just at that moment when his lance has broken and he and his horse are about to crash to the ground. Sancho, as usual, is standing by on his donkey not believing his own eyes.[23] [Fig. 6]

[1863] A drawing by the famous French illustrator Gustave Doré with Don Quixote and his horse being hurled through the air by a menacing windmill's sail and little Sancho standing next to his donkey fearing for the life of his master.[24] [Fig. 7]

[1900] An illustration by the British artist Walter Crane in an English *Don Quixote* edition. This is a rather innovative interpretation of the windmill scene in that Crane does not show Don Quixote being defeated by the windmill as the other illustrators have done. Instead, perhaps mindful of the English proverbial expression "to tilt at windmills," Crane's drawing shows Don Quixote with tilted lance as he spurs on his horse to charge the windmill as Sancho in vain attempts to stop his crazy master.[25] [Fig. 8]

But to return to the question what all of this crazy business could mean, it will surprise nobody to learn that Cervantes scholars have proposed various possible explanations in their never-ceasing studies on this great novel that is considered by some to be the *summum bonum* of this genre in world literature. There is hardly a study that does not at least refer to the windmills, with several long chapters or articles devoted exclusively

16

Figure 3

Figure 4

Figure 5

Figure 6

Figure 7

Figure 8

to them. They are all looking for "what they *mean*: what they mean to Don Quixote, and what they mean to Sancho, and why."[26] It is in principal a semiotic question that needs to be answered here, including of course also what the sign of the windmills means to the readers over time, including the modern student of Cervantes. Some of the results of these interpretive quests include the following in chronological order of their appearance:

[1971] It is little wonder [that] Don Quixote's first case of hallucination concerns a giant. The symbolism here is of some interest. Windmills are the products of civilization in its search to harness and to utilize natural power. They symbolize, ironically, the very element which Don Quixote lacks. No humanistic reason, no windmill, that is, harnesses his powers. The symbol and Don Quixote's inability to recognize it provide in one chapter the whole novel in summary.[27]

[1973] This is probably by far the most popular passage [i.e., adventure] in *Don Quixote*. Why should this be? I cannot think of any explanation but the obvious one: we have here a confrontation of man and machine, one of the earliest in literature, and one of the most perfect. [...] That means, we have the motif here already in its modern form: the confrontation with a *new* technology.[28]

[1985] Dans une minute d'inspiration il [Don Quixote] a reconnu probablement que les moulins ne sont pas des parties du paysage mais des *machines* et que toute une armée de machines se dresse autour de lui et le menace, lui et l'humanité représentée par son serviteur Sancho Panza, dans leur existence. [...] Des géants, aussi puissants et menaçants soient-ils, sont toujours infiniment préférables aux machines. [...] Prophète, il voit dans l'ascension des machines le déclin probable de l'humanité.[29]

[1990] We can assume the hidalgo had known and seen windmills on the plain of Montiel all of his life; now he sees and charges at giants. His error, simply put, is one of sight perception. [...] But a greater error is involved also, the moral one of man defiant and haughty executor of divine will: or, putting them together, the flaw of human pride on the scale of heroic exertion – excess of pride and hopeless (if not senseless) overreach.[30]

[1991] If the windmill against which Don Quixote tilts embodies the wheel of Fortune turned by Fortune's wind, it is easy to fathom why Cervantes placed that episode at the very beginning of the knight's first journey with his squire. As the novel's most memorable image, the giant windmill with its revolving vanes encapsulates the pattern of circularity that characterizes not only Fortune's wheel but also Don Quixote's whole career as a knight. The novel opens with his lapse into madness, and closes with his repossession of sanity. For each of his three sallies from home, there is a return home, and throughout his career victories are followed by defeats. [...] The novel [is] the account of one man's revolution around Fortune's wheel.[31]

[1991] Pere estas características permiten comprender mejor, además, por qué, en la mente de don Quijote, los gigantes han podido estar en relación con los molinos. En efecto, en el folklore europeo, el mundo de la molienda tiene mala fama, por estar envuelto el molino en un ruido *infernal* (el de la rueda y las muelas) y por aparecer como un centre de robo y erotismo. [...] Embestir contra los molinos o los gigantes es pues, en ambos casos, embestir contra las fuerzas del Mal.[32]

[2004] The iconic value of a man attacking a large machine, together with its strategic early placement in the novel (the 'primacy effect'), have made it [the windmill-adventure] the standard for graphic interpretations of *Don Quixote*. One definition of a quixotic character or person is one who 'tilts at windmills.' Further, the windmill, with its arms that turn round and round but go nowhere, is itself a symbol of madness (usually seen in the clown's pinwheel or the circular motion we make with our finger pointing at our temple in order to indicate craziness).[33]

These seven excerpts must suffice to present a picture of the various ways that Cervantes scholars have tried to interpret the windmills and Don Quixote's and Sancho Panza's relationship to them and to each other. Clearly there exist at least "three pairs of antithetical ideas and currents" in this uniquely paired couple of characters, i.e., "the opposition madness-sanity," "the opposition art-reality," and "the opposition between subjective-objective."[34] They can all be discerned in the two pages of the windmill-adventure which allows a multitude of interpretations that might even include an illustration of the truth and wisdom of the Bible proverb "Pride goeth before a fall" (Proverbs 16,18).[35] After all, even though Don Quixote always acts with noble intentions, he does exhibit considerable hubris in his usually unprovoked attacks and battles. In comparison to the traditional knights errant whose quests normally end in victories, Don Quixote shows himself as "the hero upside-down,"[36] i.e., the virtuous super knight cut down to human size who eventually recognizes his imperfections with melancholy, humility, and above all sanity. Sancho in one of his philosophical moments says all of this best in some comments regarding the behavior of his master: "But now I see that what they say is true: the wheel of fortune turns faster than a water wheel, and those who only yesterday were on top of the world today are down on the ground."[37] In this proverbial statement, he might as well have replaced the "water wheel" of a mill driven by a stream with the windmill of the famous early adventure. The proverbial wheel of fortune does indeed relate to the rotating windmill with both metaphors describing the ups and downs of human life.

3. Windmills and proverbial duels

Cervantes must have known that he had a good thing going with his windmill-adventure, and he certainly took care to remind his readers of this central episode from time to time by at least alluding to it. Thus he has Sancho say of one upcoming dangerous adventure that "This will be worse than the windmills,"[38] and regarding another truly challenging adventure, "Sancho, with tears in his eyes, begged his master to desist from such an undertaking, compared to which the adventure of the windmills, and that of the waterwheels, and, in short, all the feats he had performed in the entire course of his life had been nothing but child's play."[39] Early in the second half of the novel that appeared in 1615 ten years after the first part, Cervantes also includes a telling bit of information that explains the positive reaction by his contemporary readers to the windmill-adventure. When Don Quijote asks the Señor Bachelor, "which deeds of mine are praised the most," the bachelor responds that "there are different opinions, just as there are different tastes: some prefer the adventure of the windmills, which your grace thought were Briareuses and giants; others, that of the waterwheel [...]."[40] But there is also one of Sancho's revealing soliloquies, in which he once again calls on his mental "sack filled with proverbs,"[41] as Don Quixote describes his squire's predisposition to proverbs which the latter "string[s] together like beads"[42] without much rhyme or reason:

"Well now: everything has a remedy except death, under whose yoke we all have to pass, even if we don't want to, when our life ends. I've seen a thousand signs in this master of mine [Don Quixote] that he's crazy enough to be tied up, and I'm not far behind, I'm as much a fool as he is because I follow and serve him, if that old saying is true: 'Tell me who your friends are and I'll tell you who you are,' and that other one that says, 'Birds of a feather flock together.' Then, being crazy, which is what he is, with the kind of craziness that most of the time takes one thing for another, and thinks white is black and black is white, like the time he said that the windmills were giants, [...], it won't be very hard to make him believe that a peasant girl, the first one I run into here, is the lady Dulcinea; [...]."[43]

After yet another one of Sancho's proverbial diatribes, Cervantes has Don Quixote say in utter frustration:

"God and all his saints curse you, wretched Sancho," said Don Quixote, "as I have said so often, will the day ever come when I see you speak an ordinary coherent sentence without any proverbs? Señores, your highnesses should leave this fool alone, for he will grind your souls not between two but two thousand proverbs brought in as opportunely and appropriately as the health God gives him, or me if I wanted to listen to them."[44]

Much has been written on the frequent employment of proverbs in *Don Quixote*, but it would be a mistake to ridicule only Sancho for his over-reliance on proverbs.[45] Cervantes as the narrator delights in using them in the narrative flow, and he certainly places them also in Don Quixote's discourse.[46] One of the most telling of many such proverbial exchanges between master and squire takes place in chapter sixty-seven of the second part towards the end of the novel when Don Quixote has decided to become a shepherd and lead a pastoral life for a year:

"Sanchica, my daughter, [said Sancho], will bring food up to our flocks. But wait! She's a good-looking girl, and there are shepherds more wicked than simple, and I wouldn't want her to go for wool and come back shorn; love and unchaste desires are as likely in the countryside as in the cities, in shepherd's huts as in royal palaces, and if you take away the cause, you take away the sin, and if your eyes don't see, your heart doesn't break, and a jump over the thicket is better than the prayers of good men."

"No more proverbs, Sancho," said Don Quixote, "for any one of those you have said is enough to explain your thoughts; I have often advised you not to be so prodigal in your proverbs and to restrain yourself from saying them, but it seems that it is like preaching in the desert, and 'My mother punishes me, and I deceive her.'"

"It seems to me," responded Sancho, "that your grace is like the pot calling the kettle black. You reprove me for saying proverbs, and your grace strings them together two at a time."

"Look, Sancho," responded Don Quixote, "I say proverbs when they are appropriate, and when I say them they fit like the rings on your fingers, but you drag them in by the hair, and pull them along, and do not guide them, and if I remember correctly, I have already told you that proverbs are brief maxims derived from the experience and speculation of wise men in the past, and if the proverb is not to the point, it is not a maxim, it is nonsense. [...]."[47]

And sure enough, there is a humorous follow-up to this proverbial exchange just two pages later:

"I have never heard you speak, Sancho," said Don Quixote, "as elegantly as now, which leads me to recognize the truth of the proverb that you like to quote: 'It is not where you were born but who your friends are now that counts.'"

"Ah, confound it, Señor!" replied Sancho. "Now I'm not the one stringing proverbs together; they also drop two by two from your grace's mouth better than they do from mine, but between my proverbs and yours there must be this difference: your grace's come at the right time, while mine are out of place, but in fact they're all proverbs."[48]

The point of all of these and numerous other exchanges like it (especially in the second part of the novel) is to add considerable folk wisdom and a solid dose of humor to the discourses between Don Quixote and Sancho Panza, but clearly Cervantes is also satirizing the overuse of proverbs during his time. But he also has a good idea of what a proverb is, that proverbs strung together can contradict each other, and that proverbs really only make sense when applied correctly in a fitting context. And yet, he definitely is not the only literary author who ridiculed this proverb mania during the so-called golden age of the European proverbs during the sixteenth century and lasting through the first half of the seventeenth century.[49] Well-known writers like William Shakespeare, François Rabelais, and Hans Jakob Christoffel von Grimmelshausen, just to name three of them, were doing the same with much satirical wit, showing in fact a similar ambivalent stance regarding proverbs as traditional wisdom on the one hand and as folk wisdom too simple to be used by the educated elite.

4. The proverbial phrase "to have windmills in one's head"

Returning to our proverbial muttons, as it were, it is time to look at the influence that the proverbial windmill-adventure itself has had on the English language and its proverbial metaphors. Before tracing the appearance and dissemination of "to tilt at windmills" and its variants, a glance must also be cast on another proverbial phrase that had its origin in this chapter of *Don Quixote*. The phrase in question is "to have windmills in one's head" with the meaning of "to be crazy" that goes back to a statement by Sancho Panza at the end of the windmill-episode. In Edith Grossman's English translation of the short passage that was already cited above the phrase is barely discernible:

"God save me!" said Sancho. "Didn't I tell your grace to watch what you were doing, that these [the giants] were nothing but windmills, and only somebody whose head was full of them wouldn't know that?"[50]

28

Interestingly enough, Cervantes' Spanish original does not really contain a direct reference to having windmills in one's head either, as a word-by-word translation reveals:

Válame Dios! – dijo Sancho – No le dije yo a vuestra merced que mirase bien lo que hacia, que no cran sino molinos de viento, y no lo podía ignorar sino quien llevase otros tales en la cabeza?[51]
("God save me!" said Sancho. "Did I not [Didn't I] tell your grace to watch well what you were doing, that they [the giants] were only windmills, and that only someone who carried other such [windmills] in his head could not know that?")[52]

But here is what the first English translator of *Don Quixote*, Thomas Shelton, did with this passage in 1612 when the first part of the novel was published in England merely seven years after its original publication:

'Good God!' quoth Sancho, 'did I not foretell unto you that you should look well what you did, for they [the giants] were none other than windmills? nor could any think otherwise, unless he had also windmills in his brains.'[53]

It is a known fact that Shelton's translation is replete with errors and imprecisions,[54] and he certainly changed Cervantes' merely indirect reference to having windmills in one's head to a rather precise statement, in addition of changing "head" to "brains."

Even though Shelton's translation of 1612 appears not to have been a publishing success, it obviously had some influence on the British book market and its readers, especially when he published the first part in 1620 again together with his new translation of the second part of the novel. In England the windmill-chapter also caught the fancy of readers, and three years after Shelton published his complete translation his metaphorical formulation of "windmills in one's brains" found its way into Thomas Dekker's play *The Witch of Edmonton* (1623):

Then 'twas my fancy.
Some windmill in my brains for want of sleep.[55]

Sixteen years later James Shirley employed a variant in his play *The Ball* (1639), indicating the change from "brains" to "head":

I am abus'd else; nay, I do love
One that has windmills in his head.[56]

Also in 1639, the statement appears in John Clarke's *Paroemiologia Anglo-Latina or Proverbs English, and Latine* as a way of rendering the Latin concept of "Chimaera" into colloquial English: "He hath wind milnes in 's head. / Chimaera."[57] This must be taken as an indication that Shelton's statement had reached a proverbial status within less than three decades, an impressive feat indeed. And sure enough, the metaphorical phrase continued to gain currency, as can be seen from a number of additional contextualized references from the middle of the seventeenth to the end of the eighteenth century:

[1664] I'm ev'n resolv'd to follow the rest of the world – that is to say, feed the humours of fools; and if they will set up windmills in their heads, contribute my assistance to cut out the sails. (John Wilson)[58]

[1667] Faith, sir, my skill is too little to praise you as you deserve; but if you would have it according to my poor ability, you are one that had a knock in your cradle, a conceited lack-wit, a designing ass, a hair-brained fop, a confounded busy-brain, with an eternal windmill in it; this, in short, sir, is the contents of your panegyric. (John Dryden)[59]

[1705] Ignorant he [the Frenchman M. Rochbrunne] was, and half cracked, and a perfect Gascon although not of the province. He pretended to the States that he was persecuted for his religion, although he was born and bred of the Gallican Church, but he was like to most of the renegade monks that fly into England, Holland, etc., for to marry. So he did to one of the maids of honour to the Princess Nassau, Frize, who had a windmill in her head like her husband. (Thomas Bruce Ailesbury)[60]

[1749] But all of this only shows the natural unsettled humor, the rapid motion of enthusiastic heads. [...] The wind-mill is indeed in all their heads. (George Lavington)[61]

[1754] Mrs. D. is returned ill from her romantic excursion. What, what, are the best of you, at any time of life, when you have the misfortune of being freed from control? I told Mrs. D. so on this very occasion. But she had a windmill in her head, and away the air of it carried her upwards of one hundred miles from her Doctor; when but a little before, she would not trust herself above three miles from him. Upon my word, Madam, not one good woman in an hundred, is fit to be left to her own head. (Samuel Richardson)[62]

The proverbial expression also appeared in 1678 in John Ray's *Collection of Proverbs* as "To have windmills in his head,"[63] and E.B. Gent included it twelve years later in his fascinating *A New Dictionary of the Terms Ancient and Modern of the Canting Crew, in Its Several Tribes of Gypsies, Beggers, Thieves, Cheats, & with An Addition of Some Proverbs, Phrases, Figurative Speeches, , &* (1690) as "*Wind-mills in the Head*, empty Projects." [64] As the earlier references show, "having windmills in one's head" usually means that a person is a bit crazy, but here the meaning of the phrase has been expanded to include empty (i.e., crazy) projects. The 1928-entry of this phrase in the *Oxford English Dictionary* cites a similar definition: "A fanciful notion, a crotchet; a visionary scheme or project."[65] But again, the term "crotchet" with its meaning of "an odd fancy or whimsical notion" carries in it the idea of being a bit crazy. The editors of the *OED* (also of the identical entry in the 1989 second edition!)[66] appear not to have been aware of the phrase's connection with the novel of *Don Quixote*, and not having found any references of it from the nineteenth and twentieth centuries, they have marked it as being obsolete.

A glance into the standard scholarly Anglo-American proverb dictionaries presents a somewhat more complete picture, with the editors clearly making the connection with Cervantes' book and Shelton's translation. Charles N. Lurie in his collection of *Everyday Sayings* (1928) includes the following revealing statement:

A person whose head is filled with queer ideas is said sometimes to have windmills in his brain. Sancho Panza spoke up to his master, and declared that anyone who could mistake the windmills for anything else "must have had windmills in his head."[67]

31

And G.L. Apperson in his invaluable dictionary of *English Proverbs and Proverbial Phrases* (1929) actually succeeded in locating a nineteenth-century reference after all in Charles H. Spurgeon's *John Ploughman's Talk; or, Plain Advice for Plain People* (1869): "Poor soul, like a good many others he has windmills in his head, and may make his will on his thumbnail for anything that he has to give."[68] He also refers to Shelton's 1612 translation as the origin of the English phrase, and this is the case as well with a number of subsequent scholarly proverb collections that mention some of the references presented here in larger contexts.[69] Even though these collections include no references from the twentieth century, I can now cite Nick C. Ellis' title of a review from 1999 with its first sentence that alludes to the proverbial phrase under discussion: "The windmills of your mind: commentary inspired by Cervantes (1615) on [Matthew] Rispoli's review of *Rethinking innateness. – Rethinking innateness* (RI) is a quixotic book, enthusiastic and visionary."[70] Since Nick Ellis explicitly mentions that his commentary was inspired by Cervantes, he might very well have been aware of the proverbial phrase "to have windmills in one's head" in its dual meaning of being crazy or to have a fanciful vision of sorts. But he actually might also have recalled it from a popular and repeatedly recorded song with the identical title of "Windmills of Your Mind" (1968). Its words and music are by Alan Bergman and Michel Jean Legrand, and it was featured in the movie *The Thomas Crown Affair* starring Faye Dunaway and Steve McQueen. It was especially Petula Clark whose rendition made the song into a major musical hit, with the words of the first verse and the two refrains going like this:

> Round, like a circle in a spiral
> Like a wheel within a wheel.
> Never ending or beginning,
> On an ever spinning wheel
> Like a snowball down a mountain
> Or a carnival balloon
> Like a carousel that's turning
> Running rings around the moon
>
> [1. refrain]
> Like a clock whose hands are sweeping
> Past the minutes on it's [sic] face

And the world is like an apple
Whirling silently in space
Like the circles that you find
In the windmills of your mind

[2. refrain]
Like a circle in a spiral
Like a wheel within a wheel
Never ending or beginning,
On an ever spinning wheel
As the images unwind
Like the circles that you find
In the windmills of your mind[71]

In this song of love and memories, the four times repeated lines of "Like the circles that you find / In the windmills of your mind" express the incessantly turning wheels of the mind with its "crazy" visions of good times past. A bit of field research among friends and colleagues revealed that this song was indeed quite popular with people remembering especially the couplet "Like the circles that you find / In the windmills of your mind." And yet, these same people didn't necessarily know the older variant of "the windmills in your head" and were also not aware of the Cervantes connection. In fact, they were quick to point out that they would use such proverbial expressions like "to have a bee in your bonnet" or simply "to be nuts" to characterize people with strange or crazy ideas.

This must lead to the conclusion that the proverbial expression "to have windmills in one's head" that had its origin with Thomas Shelton's 1612 translation of Cervantes' *Don Quixote* must be considered defunct in today's English language. Its registration in F.P. Wilson's *The Oxford Dictionary of English Proverbs* (1970) with reference to Cervantes and Shelton is thus merely of historical value, especially since references stop with Samuel Richardson's epistolary use of it in 1754 cited above.[72] But while it is laudable that this dictionary includes the proverbial phrase "to have windmills in one's head," it is a riddle how its editor could have failed to register the much more popular and internationally disseminated proverbial phrase "to tilt at windmills" with its impressive currency still today, even though the identification and understanding of the imagery of windmills is slowly but surely waning. Proverbs and proverbial expressions come and go, and when the realia of the metaphors do not fit any longer, they will eventually drop from common usage.

5. The proverbial phrase "to fight with a windmill"

While the reception and influence of Cervantes' *Don Quixote* on the English literary scene was not overwhelming during the fifty years after its original publication and translation into English, Edwin B. Knowles was nevertheless able to locate eighty allusions to the novel in various literary texts in his invaluable dissertation on *The Vogue of "Don Quixote" in England from 1605 to 1660* (1938). Perhaps not surprisingly, *"Don Quixote* was most used, and earliest used, by dramatists, next most frequently by 'witty' writers of verses and prose ephemera,"[73] with the allusions referring primarily to humorous elements of the novel. The amazing part of all of this is, however, that Knowles discovered five allusions to *Don Quixote* before Thomas Shelton's translation was published in 1612, indicating that although only few British people of the time could read Spanish,[74] some must have read the Spanish original or gathered some knowledge about the novel through oral communication. Little wonder then that "the earliest references are commonly only to the title of the book or to the Don's name, or to windmills. They reveal little or no comprehension of Cervantes' story, or acquaintance with it."[75]

Be that as it may, the first allusion to *Don Quixote* thus far found in English literature appears in George Wilkins' play *The Miseries of Enforced Marriage* (1607), where gallant young William Scarborrow, the unhappy victim of the forced marriage, finds refuge and relief in alcohol. Perfectly drunk, he shouts to his attendant:

> Boy, bear the Torch faire: Now am I armd to fight with
> a Wind-mill, and to take the wall of an Emperor: Much drinke,
> no money: A heavy head, and a light paire of heeles.[76]

Referring to these few lines already in 1905, James Fitzmaurice-Kelly remarked:

> "To fight with a windmill!" The expression betrays its
> source; it would be unmeaning to any one unacquainted

with the eighth chapter [of *Don Quixote*] in which Cervantes describes Don Quixote's terrible adventure with the giants whom the wizard Frestón had transformed into windmills upon the plain leading to Puerto Lápice. Wilkins was not the man to write above the heads of his audiences, and he clearly believed that they would catch the point of the allusion. The experiment was evidently successful, for, in the following year, Middleton repeated it in the fourth act of *Your Fair Gallants* [...].[77]

Indeed, the well-known dramatist Thomas Middleton used the identical phrase "to fight with a windmill" one year later in his play *Your Five Gallants* (1608), where another witty gallant by the name of Pyamont rages about the loss of forty pounds:

No less than forty pounds in fair gold at one lift! the next shall swoon and swoon again till the devil fetch him, ere I set hand to him. Heart, nothing vexes me so much, but that I paid the goldsmith [i.e., banker] for the change too not an hour before: had I let it alone in the chain of silver as it was at first, it might have given me some notice at his departure: 'sfoot, I could fight with a windmill now. Sure 'twas some unlucky villain: why should he come and salute me wrongfully too, mistake me at noonday? Now I think on't it in cold blood, it could not be but an induction to some villainous purpose: well, I shall meet him —[78]

There has been some speculation on where both Wilkins and Middleton might have come across the windmill-phrase, but scholars in general agree that it must be an allusion to *Don Quixote* that they somehow picked up prior to Thomas Shelton's 1612 translation of the novel. Edwin Knowles states the following:

Although both of these allusions in all probability go back to Chapter VIII of the Spanish novel, neither bears any direct relation to that book. It is clear that though Wilkins and Middleton *may* have read *Don Quixote*, they could easily have composed this amusing remark as a result of hearing about the book. Indeed, as later examples [of allusions] bear witness, familiarity with the book would very naturally have tended to cause the addition of Don Quixote's name. Mr. Fitzmaurice-Kelly to the contrary, these allusions do not pre-suppose that the audience would recognize their source, for in each case the context is self-explanatory [and the novel was in fact little known!]; nor, for that matter, is there any evidence that Wilkins or Middleton knew who had fought with windmills. Finally, as contexts are often good indications of the author's interpretation of the references he puts in them, it should be observed that both speakers are in extravagant moods, one as the result of liquor and the other of rage.[79]

And also observe these remarks by Baldwin Maxwell from 1951 that adds the interesting aspect of a possible oral currency of the phrase to the discussion:

The allusion to *Don Quixote* is hardly enough to indicate that Middleton had read either Cervantes' original or Shelton's translation, which, although not printed until 1612, is assumed to have been under way by 1607. [...] Wilkins' and Middleton's allusions are so similar and, indeed, so inexact that one suspects neither dramatist to have known *Don Quixote* except by hearsay. [...] Similar in their suggestion that fighting with a windmill represents a stage of desperation, the two allusions carry a meaning so different from the episode in *Don Quixote* that one is led to suspect that there may have been indebtedness of one dramatist to the other. Neither, however, seems closer to Cervantes than the other, and it is of course possible that the expression "fight with a windmill" had passed into the London slang of the day. If one dramatist was here indebted to the other, the debt may well have been Middleton's.[80]

What is one to make of all these comments? It is clear that Middleton might simply have taken the windmill-phrase from Wilkins' play. But where did Wilkins really find it? He might have received it by "hearsay" from someone acquainted with the original Spanish *Don Quixote*, but it is doubtful and more likely impossible that the phrase already "had passed into the London slang of their day." Proverbial phrases did not get established that quickly at a time without the mass media and the internet.

There is, of course, another hitherto not mentioned possibility, and that is simply that George Wilkins came up with the phrase himself! After all, windmills were perfectly plentiful in England, as a reader of Edwin Knowles' unpublished dissertation also observes in a handwritten comment in the margin: "Isn't it possible that these [the two references in Wilkins and Middleton] have nothing to do with *DQ*? There were windmills in Eng."[81] The presence of windmills in England has been well researched, and it is an established fact that they existed in that country at least since the end of the twelfth century (1185 and 1191 being the earliest written references), with their primary purpose being to grind corn and to drain swamps.[82] In fact, "from the thirteenth century onwards windmills spread throughout England, and even into North Wales and Scotland, until at one time as many as ten thousand were at work in England."[83] Windmills were thus much more prevalent in England during the time of Cervantes. Indeed, when he wrote his famous windmill-adventure, "windmills were still a novelty in La Mancha, having first appeared there in 1575.[84] For Cervantes they were the beginning of a new machine age, something that makes the interpretation of the windmill-adventure as Don Quixote's human struggle against the technological threat even more plausible! The earliest windmills had, however, already appeared around 1330 in Spain.[85] In any case, with all those windmills cluttering the English landscape, it should not have been difficult for Wilkins to come up with the observation that a drunkard might be crazy enough to fight against such a gesticulating monster. Besides, it was only a very small linguistic and metaphorical step to move from the late medieval English proverbial expression "to fight against the wind" to fighting windmills. In his invaluable collection of *Proverbs, Sentences, and Proverbial Phrases from English Writings Mainly before 1500* (1968), the paremiographer Bartlett Jere Whiting cites the following reference from the *Melusine* from circa 1500: "For ye oweth to wete that wel fole is he that fighteth ayenst the wynd, wenying to make hym be styll."[86] Here then is a fool trying to stop the wind, quite similar to Don Quixote fighting against moving windmill sails. A second reference out of Nicholas Udall's *Thersytes* from around 1560 also corresponds somewhat with Don Quixote's situation: "Do not set your mynde To fyghte with the wynde."[87] What all of this means is that the English phrase "to fight with a windmill" might have originated in England independently from Cervantes' *Don Quixote*. In this regard, attention can also be drawn to a British manuscript from about 1326 kept at Christ Church College (Oxford). It contains two sketches, with the first depicting a windmill converted into a catapult, used to hurl beehives at a besieged castle [Fig. 9] and the second showing how a beehive is being hurled by that windmill into a castle.[88] [Fig. 10] In other words, there were fights with windmills going on at least in some fashion in England prior to Cervantes. However, to prove beyond any doubt that the phrase "to fight with a windmill" was known in England before Cervantes a reference would have to be found that predates the 1605 publication of *Don Quixote*. Polygenesis is certainly possible with proverbs and proverbial expressions,[89] and this might just be the case regarding the proverbial fight against windmills.

Even if George Wilkins originated his own statement "to fight with a windmill" with Thomas Middleton picking it up the following year, it must be stated that it apparently did not reach true proverbial status. For this to be the case one would have to be able to locate more references of the phrase during the following decades without any direct allusions to the *Don Quixote* novel. This is, however, hitherto not the case. In fact, the next literary reference of fighting windmills found thus far stems from 1644, that is from almost four decades later, and it contains a definite allusion to Don Quixote's windmill-adventure. John Cleveland's use of the phrase in his essay on "The Character of a Country Committee-Man, with the Ear-Mark of a Sequestrator" (1644) is thus proof positive that the expression "to fight against windmills" was definitely associated with Don Quixote by the middle of the seventeenth century:

> Thus the Quixotes of this age fight with the windmills of their own heads, quell monsters of their own creation, make plots, and then discover them; as who fitter to unkennel the fox than the terrier that is part of him?[90]

The formulation "to fight with the windmills of their own heads" seems to be a fascinating combination of the truly British proverbial phrase "to have windmills in one's head" and the allu-

Figure 9

Figure 10

sion to Don Quixote's fight with windmills that was slowly but surely becoming proverbial.

Two additional references show clearly, how the proverbial expression "to fight with windmills" continues to be associated with Don Quixote's windmill-adventure during the first half of the seventeenth century, thus indicating that the Spanish novel did in fact help to establish the phrase in the English language:

[1646] *Bookes* are the *Objects* there, and yet none ly
Like famous *Palmerin* or stout *Sir Guy*.
No doubty *Don Quixote*, like those that fight,
With *Warlike Wind mill*, and then rise up *Knight*.
(Martin Lluelyn)[91]

[1648] Some, *Gnatoes, Thrasoes* some, some in their pots
Are Mushrump Poets, some meere *Don Quixots*,
With Rams, and Wind-Milnes fight. (John Taylor?)[92]

By the eighteenth century the phrase is so well established in England as well as North America, that it no longer needs the association with Don Quixote's windmill-adventure. It is a commonly known proverbial phrase that can well stand on its own, as it were. A few contextualized texts will illustrate this fact beyond any doubt well into the twentieth century:

[1768] But we stand amazed at the sending over Men of War & Soldiers at a great expense to the Nation [i.e., England] to fight Windmills. Whenever they [the English soldiers] come, or in what Numbers, they will find the Americans as peaceable, I might say, much more so than the people of England [...]. (William Allen)[93]

[1775] Devoted madman! what inspir'd thy rage,
Who bade thy foolish muse with me engage?
Against a wind-mill would'st thou try thy might,
Against a giant would a pigmy fight?
What could thy slanderous pen with malice arm
To injure him, who never did thee harm? (Philip Freneau)[94]

[1778] I feel ashamed to argue this point [how to go about choosing magistrates] any longer. It seems like fighting, not against the wind-mill, but a butterfly; and therefore conclude with remarking on the supposed causes which betrayed the pro-

41

posers [of a certain selection method] into such unwise, and unconstitutional a proposal. (Thomas Paine)[95]

[1817] I entered the field as you justly observed like the Knight of La Mancha. The protection they will give to my house in Liverpool, that has vanished, and whither the remainder of my life will be spent in fighting windmills or gathering Rat Skins is a matter I cannot as yet determine. (Colin Robertson)[96]

[1894] Dr. Edersheim is again – so far as I am concerned – fighting a windmill. (Frederic William Farrar)[97]

[1950] Each century has brought forth guardians and champions of the English tongue who fought ceaseless, and sometimes meritorious, battles to save it from further foreign adulteration. But was it not altogether a fight against windmills, since the native tongue could not be defined with one national epithet, but had become a form of speech summed up by Daniel Defoe as "your Roman-Saxon-Danish-Norman English"? (Victor Grove)[98]

One final example must suffice to show how the proverbial phrase "to fight with a windmill" continues to be used in the modern age, sometimes also by referring directly to the novel itself. This is the case in a fascinating comment about the novel as a genre by the African American poet Nikki Giovanni in her autobiographical book *Gemini* (1971):

Literature is one of the tools white people have used for survival.
The major invention of the white man in literature is the novel. The Spanish exemplar of the form is *Don Quixote*, a big, clumsily written book about a dude fighting windmills for the love of some chick who didn't dig him. It deals with chivalry and knighthood and stuff. In other words it describes the standard for a life style that no Western man could afford to live. It is quite frankly foolish. But it is long enough to take a season to get through. With a big novel in the court and someone to read a couple of chapters a week winter would pass. The modern counterpart is the soap opera. You get a little each day and tune in tomorrow – in other words, you delay your gratification. Black people come from an oral tradition. We sat by the fire and told tales; we tended the flocks

and rapped poems. We had a beginning and an end for we didn't know what tomorrow would bring.[99]

There are various references to *Don Quixote* in the literary works of Nikki Giovanni,[100] and this statement is, of course, much more a tongue-in-cheek summary of the novel, mentioning its most famous adventure in passing. Giovanni is not so much using the proverbial phrase but is rather alluding to the windmill-chapter. But Giovanni's statement certainly is renewed proof that the *Don Quixote* novel lives on through the windmill-episode and the proverbial phrase based on it. Paremiographers have also decided that "To fight with a windmill" or "to fight windmills" are indeed proverbial phrases, and they have included them as lemmas with various references in their historical dictionaries.[101]

6. *Variants of the proverbial expression "to fight windmills"*

While the phrasing "to fight windmills" is a dominant variant, there are, as is always the case with real folklore, numerous other variants that make use of different verbs and that include either the singular or the plural form of the windmill-noun. What follows is but a small sampler of such variants, with several of them alluding to Don Quixote's windmill-adventure:

[1645] Fool! that with such dull arrows strove,
Or hoped to reach a flying dove;
For you, that are in motion still,
Decline our force, and mock our skill;
Who, like Don Quixote, do advance
Against a windmill our vain lance. (Edmund Waller)[102]

[1659] Since our arrival here [Bristol], my Lord and I, like *Don Quixote* and his *Sancho*, have done nothing but seek adventures, visiting all the Towns of remark, and enchanted Castles we could hear of, as if we intended to give the World a more exact Geography of the place, and mend *Cambdens* Map of the County: only we have charg'd no Windmills yet, nor any thing else but his purse. (Robert Loveday)[103]

[1779] Had you [Susanna Livingston] appealed to my friendship or to my gallantry, it would have been irresistible. I should have thought myself bound to have set prudence and policy at defiance, and even to have attacked *windmills* in your Ladyship's service. I am not sure, but my imagination would have gone so far, as to have fancied New York an *enchanted castle* – the three ladies, so many fair damsels, ravished from their friends and held in captivity, by the *spells* of some wicked magician. (Alexander Hamilton)[104]

[1799] [...] that the common law is the law of the United States, and that their courts have, of course, jurisdiction co-extensive with that law, that is to say, general over all cases and persons. But, great heavens! Who could have conceived in 1789, that within ten years we should have to combat such windmills! (Thomas Jefferson)[105]

[1826] In respect to the other subject, of an authorized ministry, baptism, etc., what you do know from the Bible on those subjects is enough, without ecclesiastical history and combats with windmills in the fog of distant ages. (Lyman Beecher)[106]

[1855] "You have heard him, Pen, talking in this way at his own table; but when he comes out armed *cap-à-pied*, and careers against windmills in public, don't you see that, as Don Quixote's son, I had rather the dear, brave old gentleman was at home?" (William Makepeace Thackeray)[107]

Having found such verbs as "to advance against," "to charge," "to attack," "to combat," and "to career against" in connection with windmills, one would expect that the verb "to joust at" has also been employed in keeping with the vocabulary of the knight errantry of Don Quixote. Two additional contextualized references illustrate that this is in fact the case, but it is surprising that the variant "to joust at windmills" appears to be of only recent coinage:

[1972] There was an edge to her voice and I thought, oh boy, here we go again. I moved on ahead of her, I was too beat to joust at windmills. (Tobias Wells)[108]

[1990] "Let's face it. The only death we can point to as a provable murder is the shooting of the Dean. Perhaps we are only jousting at windmills. Has that thought occurred to you?" (Gaylord Larsen)[109]

But then again, the variant "to joust at windmills" might actually be a variation of "to tilt at windmills" which at least in the modern age has become a second dominant variant of the pro-

44

verbial idea of fighting windmills. Both the "joust" and "tilt" verbs describe knightly behavior, with the first referring to the clash between two armored knights and the second to the charge of a knight with an inclined lance.

7. The proverbial phrase "To tilt at windmills"

Twentieth-century lexicographers and paremiographers have decided to consider the variant of "to tilt at windmills" as the standard version of the well-established proverbial expression. Their definitions of the phrase vary to a considerable extent, but almost all of them consider the windmill-adventure of Don Quixote to be the origin of the popular metaphor. What follows are at least a few representative examples of such dictionary entries:

[1922] Tilt against windmills, To: to undertake an absurd, impossible task. In allusion to an episode related of Don Quixote in Cervantes' romance of that title. (Albert M. Hyamson)[110]

[1928] Tilting at Windmills: To "tilt at windmills" means to make war against imaginary evils. We get the phrase from "Don Quixote," by Cervantes. [...] (Charles N. Lurie)[111]

[1928] In allusions to the story of Don Quixote tilting at windmills under the delusion that they were giants. (*Oxford English Dictionary*)[112]

[1948] To tilt at windmills. To attack imaginary foes or abuses: [a cliché since] mid C. 19-20. (Burton Stevenson)[113]

[1955] to tilt at windmills: To wage battle with chimeras; to take up the cudgels against an imaginary wrong or evil. The saying and its meaning take us to the redoubtable knight, Don Quixote, in the book of that name by Cervantes in 1605. [...]
(Charles Earle Funk)[114]

[1964] tilt at windmills: attack an imaginary foe; undertake an absurd, impossible or futile task. In allusion to the story of Don Quixote tilting at windmills under the delusion that they were giants. (Sanki Ichikawa)[115]

[1985] tilt at windmills: To combat imaginary evils, to fight opponents or injustices that are merely the figments of an overactive imagination. The allusion is to Cervantes' *Don Quixote de la Mancha*, in which the hero Don Quixote imagines the windmills he has come upon to be giants and proceeds to do battle, [...] (Laurence Urdang)[116]

[1987] tilt at windmills: [...] Almost as soon as Don Quixote was published it inspired the expression *to fight with* or *tilt at windmills*, "to combat imaginary foes or ward off nonexistent dangers." (Robert Hendrickson)[117]

[1989] To tilt at Windmills (*varied*). (Bartlett Jere Whiting)[118]

[1991] tilt at windmills, to. Meaning 'to try and overcome imaginary obstacles', from Don Quixote's belief in the novel (1605-1615) by Cervantes that windmills were giants and needed to be fought. (Nigel Rees)[119]

[1997] tilt at windmills: attack an imaginary enemy or wrong. From a story in Cervantes' *Don Quixote* (1605-1615) in which windmills were mistaken for giants. (Elizabeth Knowles)[120]

[1997] tilt at windmills: Engage in conflict with an imagined opponent, pursue a vain goal, [...]. This metaphoric expression alludes to the hero of Miguel de Cervantes' *Don Quixote* (1605), who rides with his lance at full tilt (poised to strike) against a row of windmills, which he mistakes for evil giants. (Christine Ammer)[121]

[2005] to tilt at (fight) windmills. (George B. Bryan and Wolfgang Mieder)[122]

It might be added here that the American paremiographer Bartlett Jere Whiting had registered the phrase under the variant of "to fight windmills" in his collection of *Early American Proverbs and Proverbial Phrases* (1977) that contains seven references ranging from 1768 to 1826. But with this variant losing out in popularity to the second major variant of "to tilt at windmills" during the later nineteenth century, he chose the lemma "to tilt at windmills" to reflect this shift in his later collection of *Modern Proverbs and Proverbial Sayings* (1989) that once again contains seven references, but this time from the three decades between 1943-1972.[123] This is a perfect example for the need of dictionary makers to adapt to changes in the actual wording of proverbial phrases.

But turning now to the appearance of "tilting at windmills" in literary sources and the mass media, it can be stated that it started to be used towards the middle of the nineteenth century, with the first reference thus far having been located in Edgar Allan Poe's satire *The Quacks of Helicon* (1841) in which he attacks literary critics:

> Poetical "things in general" are the windmills at which he [a critic by the name of Mr. Wilmer] spurs his Rocinante. He as often tilts at what is true as at what is false; and thus his lines are like the mirrors of the temple of Smyrna, which represents the fairest images as deformed.[124]

By mentioning the name of Don Quixote's horse, Poe is counting on his readers to make the connection to the windmill-chapter where Don Quixote and his horse fail in their battle against the "giants." In other references, the allusion to the *Don Quixote* novel is missing, indicating that the proverbial phrase "to tilt at windmills" has a life and meaning all by itself. Here are a few contextualized examples with the obvious lack of references between Poe's text from 1841 until Agatha Christie's use in 1937. Surely more references can be unearthed in due time:

[1937] "Rather eccentric, I'm afraid," said Porot. "Most of that family are. Spoilt, of course. Always inclined to tilt at windmills." He added carelessly. (Agatha Christie)[125]

[1949] Well, was he [Sir Arthur Conan Doyle] tilting at windmills? "We had no delusions," he afterwards wrote to the 'Times.' We expected no wholesome conversions. But at least we could be sure that the plea of ignorance [about the war in South Africa] could no longer be used." If he did tilt at foreign windmills, he wrecked the windmills. Many of them, far more of them than he had ever hoped, stopped grinding wheat for President Kruger. Others slowed down. (John Dickson Carr)[126]

[1952] "I don't know, and I'm not going to debate a hypothetical case. To the best of my knowledge and belief those small kids at Gramarye are well housed, well fed, and well clothed. [...] Don't go tilting at windmills, Anne." Anne suddenly grinned. "All right, but do just tell me this. What do you mean by windmills?" (E.C.R. Lorac)[127]

[1956] Was this thing really his business, after all? Was he, in returning from the turmoil of Korea to the sudden quiet of civilian life, unconsciously seeking windmills to tilt at? He had argued that with himself through the darkness and a number of cigarettes. (Ursula Curtiss)[128]

[1960] I remembered Gorde's description of Whitaker – an old man tilting at windmills. (Hammond Innes)[129]

[1962] If you had put him [Sir William Twynam] into armour with a lance in his hand he would have passed anywhere as Don Quixote, though I think he was the last person to tilt at windmills. (Leonard Woolf)[130]

[1968] He did so [handle his own problems] with considerable maturity, neither tilting at windmills nor becoming frustrated and bitter, curbing his impatience but not his enthusiasm. (Rhoda Truax)[131]

[1978] He hesitated, wondering how to avoid sounding corny. 'I just have a feeling Mike was into the sort of thing I'd like to be doing.' 'And what was that?' He shrugged and grinned. 'Tilting at windmills?' She shook her head sadly. (Paul Bryers)[132]

[1999] There being little else he could do in the circumstance, he brought in his cello and tuned up. 'I've been looking at *Don Quixote*,' he told Sarah. 'I can't play it all, but I've been working on Variation 3. Let me just play you a bit before we talk about other things.' 'Number 3, The Adventure with the Windmills,' Sarah murmured. 'Tilting at windmills. It seems appropriate, somehow.' (Morag Joss)[133]

[2000] Above all, however, his [Lord Chesterfield's] two letters of 1741 and 1749 calling for the careful avoidance of proverbs by educated and fashionable people are nothing but words spoken to the wind. Generations of scholars have taken them way too hastily at face value, when proverbs were actually employed both in a traditional and innovative way by Lord Chesterfield himself and his contemporaries on many occasions. In half-heartedly fighting their employment or in claiming that they disappeared during the 18th century from common use, both Lord Chesterfield and scholars have tilted at proverbial windmills. Poeple then and now do have recourse to common proverbs, and they use these traditional metaphors as part of the communicative art of indirection. (Wolfgang Mieder)[134]

It should be noted that but two of these nine relatively modern references mention Don Quixote as the novel's hero or his name as the title of a piece of music by Ludwig (Léon) Minkus. The literary aware person, having read Cervantes' *Don Quixote* or at least knowing about the novel, will doubtlessly think of the windmill-episode when using or being confronted by the proverbial metaphor of tilting at windmills. However, with diminishing cultural literacy, there are certainly ever more people of the modern age who understand the general meaning of tilting at windmills and who use it without giving its origin any thought whatsoever. In other words, "to tilt at windmills' can function as a literary allusion to Cervantes' *Don Quixote* or as an anonymous proverbial phrase.

This dual character of the windmill-metaphor can also be seen in four cartoons that contain the expression "to tilt at windmills" in the caption. For example, *The New Yorker* magazine included a cartoon in 1930 that shows several men from high society at a meeting of some type saying "'We have ideas. Possibly we tilt at windmills – just seven Don Juans tilting at windmills.'"[135] [Fig. 11] In addition to an indirect allusion to Don Quixote, there is also the change of his name to Don Juan that adds a certain sexual element to the message. And the number seven might just be a play on the seven dwarfs of the Snow White fairy tale, cutting these Don Juans down to rather unimportant people, as it were. A British cartoon from circa 1990 with the caption "Let's go and tilt at that windmill"[136] [Fig. 12] shows a couple passing by a windmill in their automobile. The mere image of that structure conjures up the windmill-phrase and the thought that they might just want to act it out as a bit of a game to add some spice to their lives. But there is also a cartoon from 2003 with the caption "Tilting at Windmills," with Sancho saying to Don Quixote: "War is all too real. Shouldn't our motives be."[137] [Fig. 13] In addition, the windmills are labelled as "Nuclear Arms," "Terror," and "9/11 Link," implying perhaps that Don Quixote should choose his battles based on a reality check. Finally, the electronic *Internet Weekly* featured a photomontage with the headline "Tilting at Windmills,"[138] [Fig. 14] showing modern power-generating windmills in the background and George W. Bush as Don Quixote saying to Vladimir Putin: "Sancho, We Must Charge all the Evil Windmills in the World!" At so much ignorance Putin as Sancho can only say to himself:

"And I Thought Stalin Was Nuts!" All of this certainly takes Don Quixote's windmill-adventure and the proverbial phrase alluding to it into new iconographic realms. Whether they be humorous or satirical allusions, they certainly play their part in keeping this cultural icon alive in the modern age.

This is also true for the repeated appearance of the windmill-metaphor in the news media, as can be seen from a database analysis of *The New York Times*. For the first fifty years (1852-1899) the computer search yielded 15 references, proving beyond any doubt that the phrase was current in the second half of the nineteenth century. It gained considerably in currency during the next five decades (1900-1950) with 150 occurrences, and for the next period of fifty years (1951-2000) the number of references for "tilt(ing) at windmills" reaches the staggering amount of 401 texts.[139] These are just the numbers for *The New York Times*, and obviously a LEXIS/NEXIS or GOOGLE search would yield many more texts attesting to the modern survival of the proverbial expression "to tilt at windmills." It is, of course, not possible to cite several hundred contextualized references here, but a representative example for each decade will illustrate that the phrase with and without allusion to Don Quixote and/or Cervantes is well and alive:

[1853] Mr. Clapp, of Erie, said the debate had certainly taken a wide range, [...]. He would allude to some things that have been said on this question – other things he should not attempt to reply to, for he had no ambition to ape the example of Don Quixote, and run a tilt against windmills. (January 31, 1853, p. 5)

[1862] Our cavalry might have charged in pursuit, captured half the rebel force and perhaps saved the bridges. As it was, the cavalry onslaught on the barricades, brave and determined as it was, was about as useless as a tilt against a windmill or a church steeple. (April 30, 1862, p. 5)

[1870] They know that any coalition with the Democrats only injures themselves and the cause. They have not thus far had sufficient of an organization behind them to make their opposition to the Committee's bill anything more than tilting at windmills. (April 18, 1870, p. 4)

"We have ideas. Possibly we tilt at windmills—just seven Don Juans tilting at windmills."

Figure 11

51

"Let's go and tilt at that windmill."

Figure 12

Figure 13

Figure 14

[1870] They know that any coalition with the Democrats only injures themselves and the cause. They have not thus far had sufficient of an organization behind them to make their opposition to the Committee's bill anything more than tilting at windmills. (April 18, 1870, p. 4)

[1884] The reasons for this gratifying change of opinion [concerning fraternities] are, in part, the almost total disappearance of those organizations that in the early days of college fraternities mistook the true purposes of those societies to be such as must lower the intellectual and moral tone of their members, the careful maintenance of a high standard of membership by influential fraternities, the better understanding of the fraternity system by its honest opponents, and finally the sheer exhaustion of those that heretofore have maintained a vigorous tilt at the windmill for exercise's sake, on finding that the windmill stands the attack much better than they. (February 2, 1884, p. 4)

[1899] However, with the odds somewhat against me, I make bold to break a spear [...], even though I have the very vivid intuition that it is quite as futile as tilting with a windmill. (December 16, 1899, p. BR880)

[1900] But I am justified in arguing that it is not incumbent upon this country [the United States] to tilt against windmills and to declare war against every monarchy and empire, at variance with every republic. If we must assist republics, we have plenty of chances near home – the republics of Central and South America. (March 25, 1900, p. 21)

[1911] Serious historical students do not believe that democracies are ruined entirely by corruption. In fact, corruption of manners has come to be recognized as a symptom rather than a disease of the body politics; so Mr. Hollingsworth tilts at windmills here. (July 30, 1911, p. BR473)

[1922] Pablo Casals put forward and promptly justified a new claim of distinction as symphonic conductor with an orchestra of ninety men [...] at Carnegie Hall last night. There was present an audience that in itself was a tribute to the Spanish cellist's commanding musicianship and personality. An eager public saw no Quixotic tilt with windmills in such adventure by the man whom Kreisler called "the best that draws a bow." (April 8, 1922, p. 22)

[1930] In a brief dispatch it is impossible [...] to tell how Stalin slashes at the Right and Left and refers bitingly to young Communists who are jealous of the laurels which Don Quixote won in his tilt against windmills. (April 4, 1930, p. 10

[1948] A friend of ours who became addicted to salmon fishing late in life insists that salmon fishing is a philosophical concept rather than a sport. He is convinced that those who haunt the banks of far-flung streams, clad in traditional costume and equipped with traditional gear, are groping for something eternally out of reach. In other words, like the hero of Cervantes, they are willing to tilt at the nearest windmill. (May 30, 1948, p. S7)

[1950] Collective quilt is a term over which much ink has been spilt, and I [United States High Commissioner John J. McCloy] hesitate, knowing the propensity of politicians to orate on the subject, even to mention it. There is no need to tilt at windmills. No one, least of all the people of the United States, is charging all Germans with the responsibility for Hitler's crimes. (February 7, 1950), p. 4)

[1963] This does not mean that inflation is permanently buried. But in its annual report, the Council of Economic Advisers comes close to taking this position. It criticizes the Eisenhower Administration – and the Federal Reserve Board – for continuing to tilt at the windmill of an inflation that no longer existed. (January 28, 1963, p. 16)

[1976] *11th St. Tenants Tilt With Windmill and Con Edison.*
Headline concerning an article about a new power-generating windmill with a photograph of a workman checking on it. (November 13, 1976, p. 22) [Fig. 15]

[1977] *Tilting Against Oil Drills.*
Headline concerning an article about off-shore oil drilling in the Atlantic Ocean with an accompanying caricature. (January 2, 1977, p. 254) [Fig. 16]

[1989] *Hawkins Discovers It's All In the Tilt.*
Don Quixote didn't get anywhere tilting at windmills, but consider what Andy Hawkins has achieved since he started tilting his breaking ball. In his first two starts as the Yankees' $3.6 million free agent, Hawkins allowed 15 runs and 20 hits in nine innings. In his three starts since that disastrous beginning, Hawkins

has given up three runs and 12 hits in 24.5 innings. (April 30, 1989, p. S2)

[1998] Ambassador Felix Rohatyn, whose business background often makes him chafe at governmental inertia, looks for ways in which an ambassador can make a difference. His latest tilt at bureaucratic windmills is an effort to increase the official American presence in the French regions outside the capital [Paris], where most American assets are today. (September 27, 1998, p. BU6).

Four of these sixteen excerpts from *The New York Times* refer to Don Quixote, but these more or less randomly chosen texts show that for the most part the proverbial expression "to tilt at windmills" is simply employed as a metaphorical phrase without any particular allusion to Cervantes or his novel. It should also be noted that the preposition "at" is at times replaced by "with." This is linguistically inappropriate, since one can tilt with a lance but not with a windmill! This wording most likely became acceptable in analogy to the proverbial variant "to fight with windmills." On the other hand, the two early references employing the noun "tilt" with the preposition "against" is perfectly correct, since the noun in the meaning of a joust does exist. However, the use of "tilt" as a noun appears not to occur any longer.

These linguistic oddities do not show up in the many book titles that have made use of "tilting at windmills." Here is but a small sample, again in chronological order:

[1888] Emma M. Connelly, *Tilting at Windmills. A Story of the Blue Grass Country*. Boston: D. Lothrop, 1888.

[1982] W.S. Bell, *Tilting at Windmills. Considerations on the Nature of the State*. London: Department of Geography, University College, London, 1982.

[1982] Piero Gleijeses, *Tilting at Windmills. Reagan in Central America*. Washington, D.C,: Johns Hopkins University, School of Advanced International Studies, 1982.

[1988] Charles Peters, *Tilting at Windmills. An Autobiography*. Reading, Massachusetts: Addison-Wesley, 1988.

[1995] Ravi Pawar (ed.), *Tilting at Windmills. New Welsh Short Fiction*. Cardiff: Parthian Books, 1995.

[1999] Ivan Eland, *Tilting at Windmills. Post-Cold War Military Threats to U.S. Security*. Washington, D.C.: Cato Institute, 1999.

[2001] Joseph Pittman, *Tilting at Windmills*. [A Novel]. New York: Pocket Books, 2001. [Fig. 17]

[2002] Andy Miller, *Tilting at Windmills. How I Tried to Stop Worrying and Love Sport*. London: Viking, 2002.

[2003] Brian Hibbs, *Tilting at Windmills. A Guide Towards Successful and Ethical Comics Retailing*. San Diego, California: IDW Publishing, 2003). [Fig. 18]

[2004] David Simpson, *Tilting at Windmills. The Economics of Wind Power*. Edinburgh: David Hume Institute, 2004.

[2005] Julian Branston, *Tilting at Windmills. A Novel of Cervantes and the Errant Knight*. New York: Shaye Areheart, 2005. Published in Great Britain as The Eternal Quest. London: Sceptre, 2003. [Fig. 19]

As can be seen, the standard phrasal title is simply "tilting at windmills" with an appropriate subtitle added to it. Nevertheless, the proverbial title obviously sets the stage for a book that will illustrate some kind of struggle or battle against imaginary or meaningless obstacles. The book by Brian Hibbs is of special interest since it is a collection of one hundred magazine columns that Hibbs published about comics with the title "Tilting at Windmills" during the decade from 1991 to 2002. And there is also the novel by Julian Branston with its great title *Tilting at Windmills. A Novel of Cervantes and the Errant Knight* (2005) that appeared on the American book market just as the celebrations of the 400th birthday of the publication of the first part of Cervantes' *Don Quixote* (1605) took place. "*Tilting at Windmills* is a dazzling evocation of Cervantes' life and times, and a brilliant weave of fact, fiction, and farce" (dust jacket) in which Cervantes is confronted with a real Don Quixote to boot. It is, however, doubtful that this novel will have the influence that the well-known musical *Man of La Mancha* (1965), written by Dale Wasserman with lyrics by Joe Darion and music by Mitch Leigh, had in keeping the knight errant Don Quixote alive in the cultural consciousness of modern people.

11th St. Tenants Tilt With Windmill and Con Edison

By ROBERT McG. THOMAS

The day they decided to put a windmill on the roof of the building at 519 East 11th Street was the day Consolidated Edison shut off the electricity, causing the water-heating solar collectors to overheat.

"You should have seen the steam," Travis Price recalled yesterday afternoon as he stood on the roof of the five-story, tenant-owned, tenant-rehabilitated building, listening to the three-blade turbine whir in the wind.

Just as soon as a few wires are connected, the 2,000-watt wind-driven generator will produce enough electricity to light the building's hallways and drive the pump for the energy system, which will provide 85 percent of the hot water used by the building's 11 tenants.

And that means that if Con Edison ever shuts off the electricity again (as it did during a brief payment dispute after the solar collectors were installed last winter), the pump will nevertheless keep on pumping, the water pipes under the solar collectors will not overheat and the tenants' hot water will not go up in steam.

The $4,000 windmill was paid for by a Federal grant and erected Thursday by the building's tenants and their 11th Street neighbors. It is the latest in a long line of innovations that have marked the rehabilitation of No. 519.

Seen as Rehabilitation Model

And like the others, including the solar collectors, the windmill is seen by Mr. Price and his associates on the project's Energy Task Force as a model for further rehabilitation under the project's primary innovation: sweat equity.

Sweat equity, in the parlance of the Adopt-a-Building project that is sponsoring the rehabilitation of No. 519 and a number of other buildings on the block, is the procedure under which tenants pay for the cooperative ownership of their apartments by donating labor to the rehabilitation.

And it is sweat equity, according to Mr. Price and the 11th Street project's Adopt-a-Building coordinator, Michael Freedberg, that will solve the city's underlying housing dilemma by providing "affordable housing," to low-income residents.

In the case of No. 519, whose rehabilitation is being financed by a $177,000 Federal loan (as well as a $43,000 Federal grant to provide extra insulation and the solar hot-water system), rents work out to an average of about $35 a room, according to Mr. Freedberg.

The New York Times/Neal Boenzi

Workmen checking fan operation of power-generating windmill erected on roof of building at 519 East 11th Street that already is using solar power.

Figure 15

Tilting Against Oil Drills

By MARTIN J. FELDMAN

IN 1973, the Suffolk County Legislature authorized County Executive John V. N. Klein to join with Nassau County officials in litigation to block petroleum and natural-gas drilling in the Atlantic Ocean off the Island. That authorization represented a philosophical statement of opposition, on behalf of Suffolk's 1.3 million residents, to oil drilling in Suffolk's oceanic backyard, and it generated a lawsuit that is still pending in the courts.

The passage of three years finds Suffolk's government no less opposed to drilling, philosophically, but it also finds us face to face with the inexorable progress of the petroleum giants in their quests to tap the resources lying beneath the Outer Continental Shelf. Whatever one's personal disdain may be for the oil industry's seemingly unchecked influence upon Federal energy policy, it is clear that neither moral indignation nor the prospect of potential environmental damage will foster the maturation of energy-producing alternatives in time to forestall this chapter of the energy story.

At its best, government exercises foresight; in this instance, the alternative is for Suffolk and other shoreline municipalities to tilt, Quixote-like, not against windmills but against offshore oil rigs, praying all the while for providential intervention.

In a more productive course of action, those municipalities, individually and in concert, would exercise their right to be informed, forewarned and equipped to deal with the contingencies attending large-scale oil drilling in coastal waters.

Toward that more productive end, I recently co-sponsored (with Legislators Elaine D. Adler, John J. Foley, Anthony Noto and Louis T. Howard) a resolution calling on Floyd S. Linton, the Legislature's presiding officer, to appoint an oversight committee with multiple responsibilities for offshore oil drilling.

These would include opening communication with industry groups, reviewing and establishing procedures and safeguards to minimize the threat of spills affecting Suffolk, reviewing the location and ramifications of shore facilities and means of conveyance and exploring those benefits that might accrue to Suffolk as a consequence of offshore drilling. Most significantly, this committee would also serve as a liaison with other municipalities sharing Suffolk's shoreline circumstances.

After the resolution was introduced (it was eventually passed, on Dec. 21, by a vote of 14 to 3 with one absent), I and several of my legislative colleagues were approached by Ralph G. Caso, the Nassau County Executive, and invited to discuss the possibility of regional planning and cooperation between the two counties on the issue. That discussion produced a shared contention that, notwithstanding the pendency of the Nassau-Suffolk lawsuit (and whatever its outcome), it is in the interest of both counties to proceed with contingency planning. Mr. Caso reacted favorably to the format of the proposed Suffolk committee as a general model for a regional committee.

Regrettably, Suffolk Executive Klein has elected to hold forth on the mountaining, contending that any dialogue with the oil industry will prejudice the pending lawsuit. While it is commonly acknowledged that there is an utter paucity of consistent, reliable information on offshore drilling and its implications, it is remarkable that Mr. Klein rails on with the self-assurance of a philosopher-king about those implications as if they were absolutes.

Without doubt, Mr. Klein has raised arguments worthy of consideration, arguments that are not without basis in fact. Ironically, those arguments should be a part of the proposed regional dialogue, along with all other input. Instead, they are the sum and substance of a doctrinaire soliloquy, the last stanza of which will probably have to be delivered from an Exxon drilling platform in the Baltimore Canyon.

Our meeting with Mr. Caso also produced an agreement to seek regional hearings conducted by the Congressional committee on offshore oil drilling. While Congress has been less than Olympian in its oversight of the petroleum industry, it remains the single best avenue of expression for local government in this matter, and the cultivation of a Congressional interest in the concerns of the Island is long overdue in the matter of drilling.

Only with the cooperation of Congress can we begin to obtain answers to some of the outstanding questions surrounding coastal drilling.

Questions remain as to the role of major oil firms as "agents" for Arab oil, from which we are presumably seeking independence.

Questions remain regarding the possibility of a production slowdown in the Gulf Coast region and the suggestion that it was engineered to force the East Coast situation.

These questions demand answers, and we have barely begun the process of inquiry. To the extent that offshore drilling is "inevitable," there is every justification for a maximum effort to protect the Island's interests, both environmental and economic. If pursuit of those interests involves discussion with major oil firms, that can hardly be characterized as a quid pro quo or a sellout by local government.

We offer our best wishes to the County Executive in his vigil on the courthouse steps. However, as Winston Churchill said, "A fanatic is one who can't change his mind and won't change the subject." There are others of us in county government who would prefer to cover all possibilities. ■

Figure 16

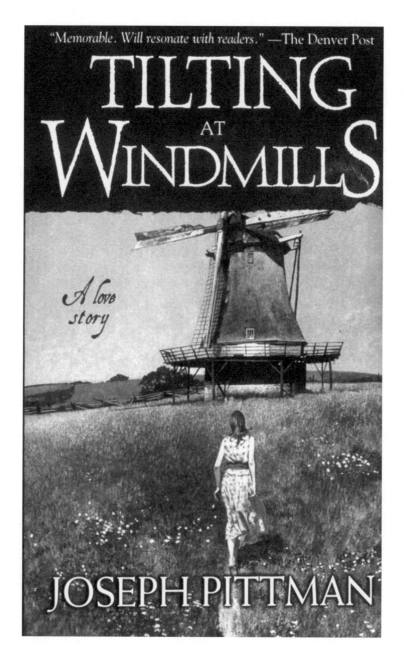

"Memorable. Will resonate with readers." —The Denver Post

TILTING AT WINDMILLS

A love story

JOSEPH PITTMAN

Figure 17

Figure 18

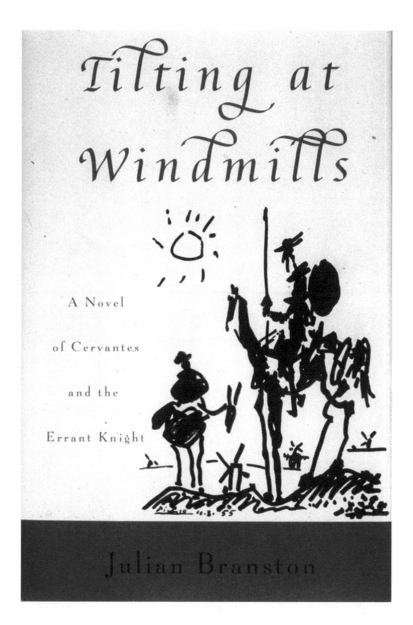

Figure 19

8. The survival of the windmill-episode in cartoons and caricatures

Despite having collected verbal and iconographic allusions to Cervantes' *Don Quixote* for three decades, only one advertisment based on the windmill-adventure has been found that comes across as somewhat of a self-caricature by the international Singer Sewing Machine Company. Singer capitalized on its ubiquitous presence in its playful international advertising, which often took landmarks or historical and literary figures, and turned them into Singer icons. One such advertisement appeared in print in Spain around 1890/1900, showing Don Quixote tilting at a windmill that has a large "S" at the center of its sails and that has the typical cast-iron footing of a sewing machine. The "S" itself exhibits the inscription "Maquinas Singer para coser" as a slogan.[140] [Fig. 20] Since everybody knows, so the reasoning of Singer must have gone, that Don Quixote will lose the fight, the message must be that Singer sewing machines are indestructible and wonderfully reliable.

Staying with business and economics, there are three German cartoons that have used the windmill-motif as telling satires. The first appeared circa 1956 and shows the German chancellor Ludwig Erhardt as Don Everyman in front of two windmills, one representing "Preise" (prices) and the other "Löhne" (wages). Not knowing how to deal with the price/wage spiral, he turns to his not illustrated squire asking: "'He, Sancho – welche soll ich zuerst besiegen?'" (Hey, Sancho, which [of these] should I conquer first?).[141] [Fig. 21] The second cartoon shows Chancellor Helmut Kohl shortly after German reunification as Don Quixote with his lance of German marks trying to deal with the vexing problems of "Soziales" (social issues), "Wirtschaft" (the economy), "Renten" (pensions), and "Arbeitslosigkeit" (unemployment), represented by the four sails of the windmill that needs to be conquered. [142] [Fig. 22] And again, the implication is, of course, that he cannot possibly succeed. The image of the third cartoon illustrates the "Attacke" (attack) of two politicians as Don Quixote and Sancho on a motorcycle and a scooter against the unpopular "Öko-Steuer" (environmental tax).[143] [Fig. 23]

The message by implication is once again that they will not be successful in their adventure. In fact, the cartoon satirizes the

Figure 20

German conservatives who do not show enough commitment to environmental issues. The windmill-motif has also been utilized to comment satirically on political issues. *The New Yorker* presented a fascinating cartoon in 1944 showing two American soldiers facing a field of Dutch windmills. One of them exhibits its four sails in the shape of a swastika, and the caption has one of the soldiers state: "'Collaborationists, probably'."[144] [Fig. 24] The allusion to the windmill-adventure might be somewhat intangible, but one could interpret the two soldiers as Don Quixote and Sancho having difficulties in distinguishing between Dutch citizens occupied by the Nazis and Dutch sympathizers co-operating with the German forces. And a Swiss cartoon from 1980 showed Don Quixote with a banner reading "Menschenrechte" (human rights) and Sancho approaching Leonid Brezhnev in a mill that has been transformed into a weapons' arsenal. The caption has Brezhnev declare the Soviet insistence on not wanting any interference in its domestic policies: "Wenn Sie mit mir verhandeln wollen, dann kommen Sie gefälligst unbewaffnet!" (If you want to negotiate with me, then at least come without weapons).[145] [Fig. 25] This is indeed an effective way to satirize the abuse of human rights during the Soviet time, showing that the fight against the overpowering machinery of Soviet might will unfortunately prove to be futile.

There are also two *New Yorker* cartoons from the 1980s that look at windmills as modern machines. One of them has a perplexed Don Quixote confront what appears to be a power-generating windmill of sorts with the following thoughts going through his troubled head: "As I grew near, the ambiguous nature of my quest became clearer. If the windmills were in fact a viable alternative energy source, I would be cursed and reviled by all of my countrymen! If, on the other hand, as I suspected, the windmills were merely another chimerical force held out to an unsuspecting public by the cynical powers that might be, every poet and minstrel in the land would sing my praises. The dilemma unresolved in my mind, I rode forward ..."[146] [Fig. 26]

Don Jedermann

„He, Sancho — welche soll ich zuerst besiegen?"

Figure 21

67

Figure 22

Figure 23

"Collaborationists, probably."

Figure 24

Madrid.

«Wenn Sie mit mir verhandeln wollen, dann kommen Sie
gefälligst unbewaffnet!»

Figure 25

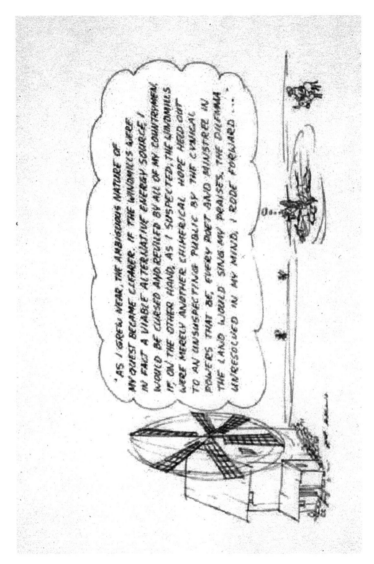

Figure 26

72

The pros and cons of windmill-energy are certainly of considerable concern still today, with people wondering whether they are useful machines or giants disgracing the natural landscape. The second cartoon is a cover illustration of the August 15, 1988, issue of *The New Yorker*. It simply shows a round electric fan in the summer heat in a desolate area with a "hot" Don Quixote and Sancho facing it.[147] [Fig. 27] Even though Don Quixote is tilting his lance, one might perhaps assume that he will not charge the fan, the only possible relief to escape what appears to be an unbearable heat wave.

There are, of course, also humorous cartoons that represent reversals of the actual windmill-episode. They demand a definite acquaintance with this adventure, or they really do not make much sense at all. Thus a *New Yorker* cartoon from 1974 shows what might be Don Quixote in front of a line-up of several other would-be knights errant giving them instructions on how to fight successfully against windmills: "So, you see, it's mainly a matter of timing and footwork."[148] [Fig. 28] And sure enough, there is a windmill that has in fact been successfully wrecked with others standing in the background waiting to be attacked. Three years later *The New Yorker* featured a funny cartoon showing Don Quixote appearing on the horizon tilting his lance. One of two windmills in the foreground, both with faces expressing dismay, can only exclaim to the other: "'En garde! A nut!'"[149] [Fig. 29]. And there is also a third cartoon from 1979 found in the British *Punch* magazine with Don Quixote and Sancho confronting what appears to be the giant Briareus whom Quixotes had mentioned in his famous windmill-adventure. But this time the deranged knight says to his scared squire: "'Godammit, Sancho, it's just a little old windmill'."[150] [Fig. 30] This cartoon certainly would not make any sense whatsoever to viewers unacquainted with the *Don Quixote* novel. Knowing the proverbial phrase "to tilt at windmills" would also not help to understand the image in this case.

Not all cartoons demand that amount of precise knowledge of Cervantes' *Don Quixote*, but they are nevertheless assuming that viewers will recognize that they allude to the windmill-chapter. In 1970, in the early days of the women's liberation movement, a cartoon appeared in *The New Yorker* without any caption showing a female Don Quixote (Gloria Steinem) and a female Sancho (Bella Abzug) calmly and self-assuredly approaching a windmill. And Señora Quixote does not tilt her lance either, implying most likely that she is not so crazy as to attack a windmill when she sees one.[151] [Fig. 31] In other words, she is not as crazy or stupid as her male counterpart and knows better how to deal with the real world. And how different was in fact the cartoon that appeared in *Punch* not quite four weeks later! Here the males Don Quixote and Sancho stand in front of a towering windmill with the noble but unrealistic Don Quixote explaining to his faithful but simple-minded squire: "'We must wait for a wind – I do not wish to stand accused of unprovoked aggression'."[152] [Fig. 32] Not quite two years later *Punch* included another humorous cartoon with Don Quixote tilting at a windmill and Sancho proudly explaining to an on-looker: "'Of course this is just a warm-up for his title fight with the Empire State building'."[153] [Fig. 33] And why should Don Quixote not also be transformed into a golf-playing knight errant? A cartoon from around 1990 shows him on his horse with a golf club in his hand about to hit a golf ball at a windmill.[154] [Fig. 34] This scene of "crazy golf" was repeated in similar fashion in *The New Yorker* in 1993, but this time Don Quixote has dismounted from Rocinante and is ready to hit the ball into the direction of a distant windmill, with Sancho true to form having been transformed into his loyal caddie.[155] [Fig. 35] Golf-lovers certainly didn't need a caption to understand these cartoons. Finally, there is one more colorful full-page cartoon that *The New Yorker* featured in the summer of 1993 in the middle of outside-barbecuing time! The caption simply states "Don Quixote in the Hamptons" and shows the knight errant on yet another bizarre adventure with his lance serving as the skewer for the meat to be grilled charging on his horse at an innocent outdoor grill with Sancho running up with a bag of charcoals.[156] [Fig. 36]

What other adventures might Don Quixote perform in the modern world? The possibilities are endless, of course, and many more *Don Quixote* novels could be written about the knight errant and his squire on their noble but peculiar adventures. Since times have changed since the first appearance of Cervantes' novel in 1605/1615, they would not necessarily have to ride on a horse and donkey any longer. A couple of motorcycles might do just as well, making Don Quixote and Sancho into easy riders of sorts. This was already illustrated in a 1977 cartoon in the *Saturday Review* with Don Quixote riding proudly along with his lance and Sancho on a smaller bike in tandem.[157] [Fig. 37] And there is finally also a 1998 *New Yorker* cartoon that shows Don Quixote with tilted lance and Sancho following him with microphone and camera to record the next adventure live.[158] [Fig. 38] They are still on animals and not in jet planes, but the message is clear. There will always be quixotic adventures in life worthy of recording and to be carried forward for posterity.

Don Quixote's and Sancho's celebrated adventure with the windmills has become a cultural icon during the four hundred years since it was conceived by Cervantes. It has withstood the test of time as a universal image of humankind's idealistic struggles in making this world a better place. Just like Don Quixote, people will tilt at imaginary windmills, sometimes for good and at other occasions for ridiculous reasons. And yet, they might nevertheless be the better for having tried to uphold utopian ideals in the face of depressing banality. In any case, the windmill-adventure has appropriately been compressed into the proverbial expression "to tilt at windmills," giving people the verbal tool to refer to their at times quixotic undertakings. Permeating all walks of life and modes of expression, the image and phrase of tilting at windmills will live on in a culturally literate environment, but a metaphorical phrase cannot possibly and should not replace the importance of reading Miguel de Cervantes Saavedra's novel *Don Quixote de la Mancha* as one of the greatest achievements of world literature.

Figure 27

"So, you see, it's mainly a matter of timing and footwork."

Figure 28

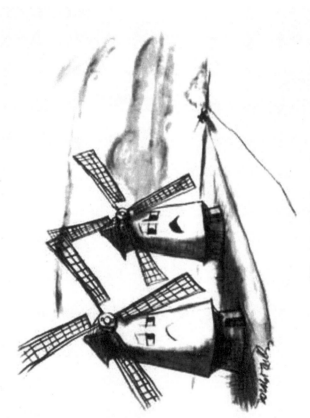

"En garde! A nut!"

Figure 29

"Godammit, Sancho, it's just a little old windmill."

Figure 30

79

Figure 31

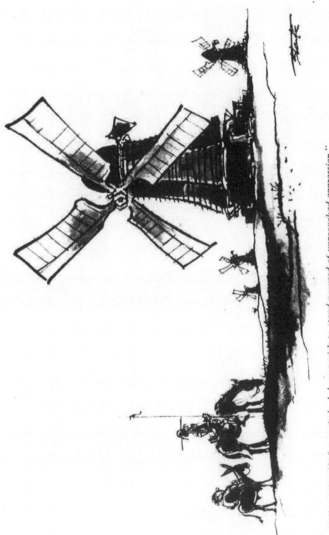

"We must wait for a wind—I do not wish to stand accused of unprovoked aggression."

Figure 32

81

82

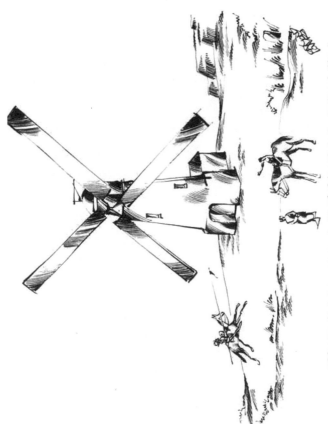

"Of course this is just a warm-up for his title fight with the Empire State building."

Figure 33

Figure 34

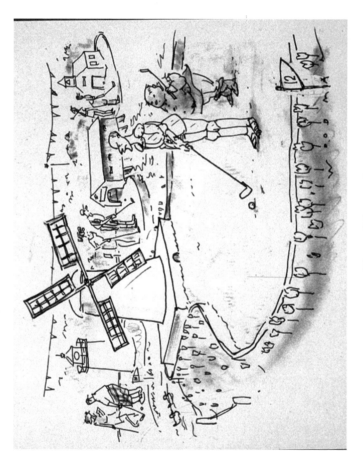

Figure 35

DON QUIXOTE IN THE HAMPTONS

Figure 36

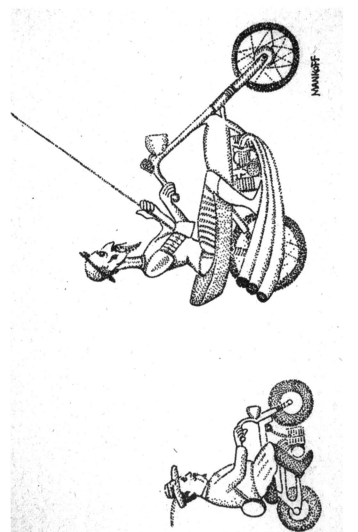

Figure 37

Figure 38

Notes:

[1] See Archer Taylor, *The Proverb* (Cambridge, Massachusetts: Harvard University Press, 1931; rpt. ed. by Wolfgang Mieder. Bern: Peter Lang, 1985), pp. 27-65; Lutz Röhrich and W. Mieder, *Sprichwort* (Stuttgart: Metzler, 1977), pp. 28-32 and pp. 83-89; and W. Mieder, *Proverbs. A Handbook* (Westport, Connecticut: Greenwood Press, 2004), pp. 9-13.

[2] See the short entry in E.D. Hirsch, Joseph F. Kett, and James Trefil, *The Dictionary of Cultural Literacy* (Boston: Houghton Mifflin Company, 1988), p. 89.

[3] See Adrien Jean Victor Le Roux de Lincy, *Le livre des proverbes français* (Paris: Paulin, 1842; rpt. Paris: Hachette Livre, 1996), p. 610; and Alain Rey and Sophie Chantreau, *Dictionnaire des expressions et locutions* (Paris: Dictionnaires Le Robert, 1993), p. 533.

[4] See Karl Friedrich Wilhelm Wander, *Deutsches Sprichwörter-Lexikon* (Leipzig: F.A. Brockhaus, 1867-1880), vol. 5, col. 266, no. *7; and Lutz Röhrich, *Das große Lexikon der sprichwörtlichen Redensarten* (Freiburg: Herder, 1991-1992), vol. 3, p. 1735.

[5] Pieter Jacob Harrebomée, *Spreekwoordenboek der Nederlandsche Taal* (Utrecht: Kemink, 1858-1870), vol. 2, p. 95 and p. 471; and F.A. Stoett, *Nederlandsche spreekwoorden, uitdrukken en gezegden* (Zutphen: Thieme, 1923), p. 509.

[7] A.V. Kunin, *Anglo-russkii frazeologicheskii slovar'* (Moskva: Gosudarstvennoe Izdatel'stvo Inostrannykh i Natsional'nykh Slovarei, 1956), p. 1193; and Sophia Lubensky, *Russian-English Dictionary of Idioms* (New York: Random House, 1995), p. 356.

[7] See Gyula Paczolay, *Ezër magyar közmondás és szólás / 1000 Hungarian Proverbs* (Budapest: Bárczi Géza Kiejtési Alapítvány, 2005), p. 116, no. 856.

[8] For references see Jacob and Wilhelm Grimm, *Deutsches Wörterbuch* (Leipzig: S. Hirzel, 1960), vol. 14, col. 314.

[9] For these Spanish variants see W. Gurney Benham, *Putnam's Complete Book of Quotations* (New York: G.P. Putnam's Sons, 1926), p. 716a; Carol Styles Carvajal and Jane Horwood, *The Spanish Oxford Dictionary, Spanish-English, English-Spanish* (Oxford: Oxford University Press, 1996), p. 420; and corpusdelespanol.org under "molinos de viento." I thank Alejandro Lee (Los Angeles) for two of these references.

[10] Cited from Miguel de Cervantes, *Don Quixote*, translated by Edith Grossman (New York: HarperCollins, 2003), pp. 58-59.

[11] Cervantes, *Don Quixote*, p. 575.

[12] Cervantes, *Don Quixote*, p. 849.

[13] For these and more characteristic elements of Quixote's adventures see Howard Mancing, *The Chivalric World of "Don Quixote". Style, Structure, and Narrative Technique* (Columbia, Missouri: University of Missouri Press, 1982), pp. 46-48 and pp. 112-114.

[14] Cervantes, *Don Quixote*, p. 21.

[15] Arturo Serrano-Plaja, *"Magic" Realism in Cervantes. "Don Quixote" as Seen Through "Tom Sawyer" and "The Idiot"* (Berkeley, California: University of California Press, 1970), p. 107.

[16] Mancing, *The Chivalric World of "Don Quixote,"* p. 48.

[17] Carroll B. Johnson, *Don Quixote. The Quest for Modern Fiction* (Boston: Twayne Publishers, 1990), p. 49.

[18] Cited from Johannes Hartau, *Don Quijote in der Kunst. Wandlungen einer Symbolfigur* (Berlin: Gebrüder Mann, 1987), p. 20 (ill. 6).

[19] Hartau, *Don Quijote in der Kunst*, p. 32 (ill. 23).

[20] Hartau, *Don Quijote in der Kunst*, p. 118 (ill. 103).

[21] Cited from Juan Givanel Mas y Gaziel, *Historia gráfica de Cervantes y del Quijote* (Madrid: Editorial Plus-Ultra, 1946), p. 474 (plates 7 and 8).

[22] Hartau, *Don Quixote in der Kunst*, p. 163 (ill. 125).

[23] Cited from H.S. Ashbee, *An Iconography of Don Quixote, 1605-1895* (London: Bibliographical Society, 1895), p. 91.

[24] Givanel Mas y Gaziel, *Historia gráfica de Cervantes y del Quijote*, p. 229 (ill. 118).

[25] Givanel Mas y Gaziel, *Historia gráfica de Cervantes y del Quijote*, p. 282 (ill. 155).

[26] Johnson, *Don Quixote. The Quest for Modern Fiction*, p. 93.

[27] Margaret Church, *Don Quixote: The Knight of La Mancha* (New York: New York University Press, 1971), p. 12.

[28] Robert Plank, "Quixote's Mills: The Man-Machine Encounter in S[cience] F[iction]," *Science Fiction Studies*, 1 (1973), 68-78 (here p. 69).

[29] Rudolf Malter, "Le moulin comme machine imaginaire. Réflexions philosophiques sur l'angoisse de l'homme dans le monde de la technique (en partant de Cervantes et de Wilhelm Busch)," *Les études philosophiques*, no volume given, no. 1 (1985), 113-124 (here pp. 113-114).

[30] L.A. Murillo, *A Critical Introduction to "Don Quixote"* (New York: Peter Lang, 1990), P. 42.

[31] Eric J. Ziolkowski, "Don Quijote's Windmill and Fortune's Wheel," *Modern Language Review*, 86 (1991), 885-897 (here pp. 896-897).

[32] Augustin Redondo, "Nuevo examen del episodio de los molinos de viento (*Don Quijote*, I, 8)," in James A. Parr (ed.), *On Cervantes. Essays for L.A. Murillo* (Newark, Delaware: Juan de la Cuesta, 1991), pp. 189-205 (here p. 199).

[33] Howard Mancing, "Windmills [Molinos de viento]," in H. Mancing, *The Cervantes Encyclopedia* (Westport, Connecticut: Greenwood Press, 2004), vol. 2, pp. 779-780 (here p. 779).

[34] Manuel Durán, *Cervantes* (New York: Twayne Publishers, 1974), p. 126.

[35] This proverb is also mentioned in Ziolkowski, "Don Quijote's Windmill and Fortune's Wheel," p. 893.

[36] See J.M. Sobré, "Don Quixote, the Hero Upside-Down," *Hispanic Review*, 44 (1976), 127-141.

[37] Cervantes, *Don Quixote*, p. 410.

[38] Cervantes, *Don Quixote*, p. 62.

[39] Cervantes, *Don Quixote* p. 562.

[40] Cervantes, *Don Quixote* p. 475.

[41] Cervantes, *Don Quixote* p. 736.

[42] Cervantes, *Don Quixote*, p. 192.

[43] Cervantes, *Don Quixote*, pp. 515-516.

[44] Cervantes, *Don Quixote*, p. 686.

[45] See especially the two newer paremiological studies by Maria Cecilia Colombi, *Los refranes en el Quijote: texto y contexto* (Potomac, Maryland: Scripta Humanistica, 1989); and Jesús Cantera Ortiz de Urbina, Julia Sevilla Muñoz, and Manuel Sevilla Muñoz, *Refranes, otras paremias y fraseologismos en "Don Quijote de la Mancha"* (Burlington, Vermont: The University of Vermont, 2005). For many additional publications see Wolfgang Mieder and George B. Bryan, *Proverbs in World Literature: A Bibliography* (New York: Peter Lang, 1996), pp. 63-67 (nos. 617-653).

[46] For some additional revealing proverbial references in the novel see Cervantes, *Don Quixote*, pp. 90, 115, 153, 165, 256, 478, 495, 498-499, 514, 528, 579, 620, 646, 654, 720, 733-736, 893, and 924.

[47] Cervantes, *Don Quixote*, pp. 901-902.

[48] Cervantes, *Don Quixote*, p. 904.

[49] See James Obelkevich, "Proverbs and Social History," in Wolfgang Mieder (ed.), *Wise Words. Essays on the Proverb* (New York: Garland Publishing, 1994), pp. 211-252 (esp. pp. 226-229).

[50] Cervantes, *Don Quixote*, p. 59.

[51] Miguel de Cervantes Saavedra, *Don Quijote de la Mancha*, ed. by Martin de Riquer (Barcelona: Editorial Juventud, 1958), vol. 1, p. 82.

[52] This translation was provided to me by my colleague and friend Prof. Timothy Murad of the Department of Romance Languages at the University of Vermont.

[53] Miguel de Cervantes, *The History of the Valorous and Witty Knight-Errant Don Quixote of the Mancha*, translated by Thomas Shelton (New York: Charles Scribner's Sons, 1906), vol. 1, p. 94.

[54] See Gustav Becker, *Die Aufnahme des Don Quijote in die englische Literatur (1605-c. 1770)* (Berlin: Mayer & Müller, 1906), pp. 6-8; and Edwin B. Knowles, *The Vogue of "Don Quixote" in England from 1605 to 1660* (Diss. New York University, 1938), pp. 284-286.

[55] Thomas Dekker, John Ford, and William Rowley, *The Witch of Edmonton*, ed. by Arthur F. Kinney (London: A. & C. Black, 1998), p. 93 (act 4, scene 2, lines 84-85).

[56] James Shirley, *Dramatic Works and Poems*, ed. by Alexander Dyce (London: John Murray, 1833), vol. 3, p. 28 (act 2, scene 3).

[57] John Clarke, *Paroemiologia Anglo-Latina or Proverbs English, and Latine* (London: Felix Kyngston, 1639), p. 158.

[58] John Wilson, "The Projectors," in *The Dramatic Works of John Wilson*, ed. by James Maidment (Edinburgh: William Paterson, 1874), p. 220.

[59] John Dryden, "Sir Martin Mar-All," in *The Works of John Dryden*, ed. by Sir Walter Scott (Edinburgh: William Paterson, 1883), vol. 3, p. 53 (act 4, scene 1).

[60] *Memoirs of Thomas, Earl of Ailesbury* (Westminster: Nichols and Sons, 1890), vol. 2, p. 576.

[61] Bishop Lavington, *The Enthusiasm of Methodists and Papists*, ed. by Rev. R. Polwhele (London: Whittaker, Sherwood and Co., 1820), p. 18.

[62] *The Correspondence of Samuel Richardson*, ed. by Anna Laetitia Barbauld (London: R. Phillips, 1804), vol. 3, p. 212.

[63] Cited from Henry G. Bohn, *A Hand-Book of Proverbs Comprising an Entire Republication of Ray's Collection of English Proverbs, with His Additions from Foreign Languages* (London: Bell & Daldy, 1870), p. 183.

[64] E.B. Gent, *A New Dictionary of the Terms Ancient and Modern of the Canting Crew, in Its Several Tribes of Gypsies, Beggers, Thieves, Cheats, & with An Addition of Some Proverbs, Phrases, Figurative Speeches, &* (London: Smith, Kay & Co., 1690), no pp. (alphabetically under "WI").

[65] *A New English Dictionary on Historical Principles* (Oxford: Clarendon Press, 1928), vol. 10, p. 164.

[66] See *The Oxford English Dictionary*, 2nd ed. (Oxford: Clarendon Press, 1989), vol. 20, p. 382.

[67] Charles N. Lurie, *Everyday Sayings. Their Meanings Explained, Their Origins Given* (New York: G.P. Putnam's Sons, 1928), p. 331.

[68] Charles H. Spurgeon, *John Ploughman's Talk; or, Plain Advice for Plain People* (New York: Sheldon & Company, 1869), p. 102 (in a short essay on "Hope," see pp. 98-104). Also cited in G.L. Apperson, *English Proverbs and Proverbial Phrases. A Historical Dictionary* (London: J.M. Dent, 1929), p. 692; and Burton Stevenson, *The Home Book of Proverbs, Maxims, and Famous Phrases* (New York: Macmillan, 1948), p. 2516 (no. 8).

[69] See Stevenson, *The Home Book of Proverbs, Maxims, and Famous Phrases*, p. 2516 (no. 8); Morris Palmer Tilley, *A Dictionary of the Proverbs in England in the Sixteenth and Seventeenth Centuries* (Ann Arbor, Michigan: University of Michigan Press, 1950), p. 730 (W455); Ivor H. Evans (ed.), *Brewers's Dictionary of Phrase and Fable* (New York: Harper & Row, 1970), p. 1159; Laurence Urdang, Walter W. Hunsinger, and Nancy LaRoche (eds.), *Picturesque Expressions: A Thematic Dictionary* (Detroit, Michigan: Gale Research Company, 1985), p. 350; Robert Hendrickson, *The Facts on File Encyclopedia of Word and Phrase Origins* (New York: Facts on File Publications, 1987), p. 525; and P.R. Wilkinson, *Thesaurus of Traditional English Metaphors* (London: Routledge, 1992), p. 161.

[70] Nick C. Ellis, "The Windmills of Your Mind: Commentary Inspired by Cervantes (1615) on Rispoli's Review of *Rethinking Innateness*," *Journal of Child Language*, 26 (1999), 232-236 (here p. 232). The book under review is by J. Elman et al., *Rethinking Innateness: A Connectionist Perspective on Development* (Cambridge, Massachusetts: MIT Press, 1996).

[71] I thank my student Erin Regan for locating this song on the internet at htpp://www.poplyrics.net/waiguo/sting/104.htm. The song might also have influenced the German poet Ulla Hahn to conclude her poem "Im Kopf" (In the Head) with the following two lines: "Und immer schneller / die Windmühlen-flügel in meinem Kopf" (And ever faster / the windmill sails in my head); see Ulla Hahn, *Galileo und zwei Frauen. Gedichte* (Stuttgart: Deutsche Verlags-Anstalt, 1997), pp. 53-54. The proverbial phrase "to have windmills in one's head" does not exist in German or other languages, as far as I know, and it is

thus a truly Anglo-American phenomenon with its occurrence in Great Britain far outweighing that in the United States.

[72] F.P. Wilson, *The Oxford Dictionary of English Proverbs* (Oxford: Clarendon Press, 1970), p. 894.

[73] Edwin Knowles, *The Vogue of "Don Quixote" in England from 1605 to 1660*, p. 214. For some of the larger uses of *Don Quixote* see also Edwin B. Knowles, "Cervantes and English Literature," in Angel Flores and M.J. Benardete (eds.), *Cervantes Across the Centuries* (New York: The Dryden Press, 1947), pp. 267-293; and Edward M. Wilson, "Cervantes and English Literature of the Seventeenth Century," *Bulletin Hispanique*, 50 (1948), 27-52.

[74] See Edwin B. Knowles, "Allusions to *Don Quixote* before 1660," *Philological Quarterly*, 20 (1941), 573-586 (here p. 573).

[75] Knowles, "Allusions to *Don Quixote* before 1600," pp. 583-584.

[76] George Wilkins, *The Miseries of Enforced Marriage* (London: George Vincent, 1607; rpt. London: The Malone Society Reprints, 1963), no pp. given (act 3, scene 7, lines 1468-1470).

[77] James Fitzmaurice-Kelly, *Cervantes in England* (Oxford: Oxford University Press, 1905), pp. 7-8.

[78] *The Works of Thomas Middleton*, ed. by A.H. Bullen (London: J.C. Nimno, 1885-1886; rpt. New York: AMS Press, 1964), vol. 3, pp. 216-217 (act 4, scene 7, lines 1-12). Archer Taylor does not include the windmill-phrase in his "Proverbs and Proverbial Phrases in the Plays of Thomas Middleton," *Southern Folklore Quarterly*, 23 (1959), 79-89.

[79] Knowles, *The Vogue of "Don Quixote" in England from 1605 to 1660*, pp. 20-21.

[80] Baldwin Maxwell, "Thomas Middleton's *Your Five Gallants*," *Philological Quarterly*, 30 (1951), 30-39 (here pp. 37-38). See also the comments by C. Lee Colegrove (ed.), *A Critical Edition of Thomas Middleton's "Your Five Gallants"* (New York: Garland Publishing, 1979), pp. 328-329 (the actual reference from the play is on pp. 141-142).

[81] Knowles, *The Vogue of "Don Quixote" in England from 1605 to 1660*, p.20 (anonymous handwritten comment in margin).

[82] See Jannis C. Notebaart, *Windmühlen. Der Stand der Forschung über das Vorkommen und den Ursprung* (Den Haag: Mouton, 1972), pp. 79-91 (chapter on windmills in England); and Suzanne Beedell, *Windmills* (New York: Charles Scribner's Sons, 1975), p. 13. See also Klaus Rockenbach, "Von der alten Windmühle. Typen, Herkunft, Denkmalpflege, Volkskunde, Dichtung," *Archiv für Kulturgeschichte*, 50 (1968), 135-153.

[83] R.J. Brown, *Windmills of England* (London: Robert Hale, 1976), p. 13.

[84] D.B. Wyndham Lewis, *The Shadow of Cervantes* (London: Hollis & Carter, 1962), 12.

[85] Notebaart, *Windmühlen. Der Stand der Forschung über das Vorkommen und den Ursprung*, pp. 193-199 (chapter about Spanish windmills). See also the excellent Spanish treatises by Efrén Fernández Lavandera and Carmelo-Millán Fernández Rodríguez, *Los molinos: Patrimonio industrial y cultural* (Vélez Málaga y Sabero: Grupo Editorial Universitario, 1997), esp. pp. 55-73; Juan Jiménez Ballesta, *Molinos de viento en Castilla-La Mancha* (Piedrabuena: Ediciones Llanura, 2001), esp. pp. 13-20, and Josi Ignacio Rojas-Sola and Juan

Manuel Amezcua-Ogayar, "Origen y expansisn de los molinos de viento en España," *Interciencia*, 30 (2005), 24 pp. (electronic version). I owe this final reference to my Spanish friend Tania Arias Vink.

[86] Bartlett Jere Whiting, *Proverbs, Sentences, and Proverbial Phrases from English Writings Mainly before 1500* (Cambridge, Massachusetts: Harvard University Press, 1968), p. 646 (W320).

[87] Tilley, *A Dictionary of the Proverbs in England in the Sixteenth and Seventeenth Centuries*, p. 728 (W431).

[88] Cited from Edward J. Kealey, *Harvesting the Air. Windmill Pioneers in Twelfth-Century England* (Berkeley, California: University of California Press, 1987), pp. 126-127.

[89] See Wolfgang Mieder, *Proverbs Are Never Out of Season. Popular Wisdom in the Modern Age* (New York: Oxford University Press, 1993), p. 174.

[90] Henry Norley (ed.), *Character Writings of the Seventeenth Century* (London: George Routledge, 1891), pp. 298-313 (here pp. 308-309).

[91] *A Critical Edition of Martin Lluelyn's Men-Miracles with Other Poems*, ed. by Robert Guy Voight (Diss. University of Arkansas, 1972), p. 93. The lines are from a poem entitled "To my Lady Chicheley," pp. 92-94.

[92] Cited from Knowles, "Allusions to *Don Quixote* before 1660," p. 578. I was unable to locate this reference in the works of John Taylor available to me.

[93] *Extracts from Chief Justice William Allen's Letter Book*, ed. by Lewis Burd Walker (Pottsville, Pennsylvania: Standard Publication Co., 1897), p. 75. The letter is dated October 29, 1768, addressed to David and John Barclay, see pp. 74-76.

[94] *The Poems of Philip Freneau. Poet of the American Revolution*, ed. by Fred Lewis Pattee (New York: Russell & Russell, 1963), vol. 1, pp. 206-207. The poem is entitled "Mac Swiggen. A Satire," see pp. 206-211.

[95] Thomas Paine, "A Serious Address to the People of Pennsylvania on the Present Situation of Their Affairs," in Philip S. Foner (ed.), *The Complete Writings of Thomas Paine* (New York: The Citadel Press, 1945), vol. 2, pp. 277-302 (here p. 301).

[96] *Colin Robertson's Correspondence Book, September 1817 to September 1822*, ed. by E.E. Rich and R. Harvey Fleming (London: Champlain Society for the Hudson's Bay Record Society, 1939), p. 10. The letter is dated October 25, 1817, and addressed to Peter Irving, brother of Washington Irving, see pp. 9-15.

[97] Cited from the *Oxford English Dictionary*, vol. 10, p. 164. I was not able to locate this reference in the edition of Frederic William Farrar's *The Life of Christ* (1874) available to me.

[98] Victor Grove, "The Indivisibility of the English Language," in V. Grove, *The Language Bar* (New York: Philosophical Library, 1950), pp. 97-108 (here p. 97).

[99] Nikki Giovanni, *Gemini. An Extended Autobiographical Statement on My First Twenty-Five Years of Being a Black Poet* (Indianapolis, Indiana: Bobbs-Merrill Company, 1971), p. 94.

[100] See Effie J. Boldridge, "Windmills or Giants? The Quixotic Motif and Vision in the Poetry of Nikki Giovanni," *Middle-Atlantic Writers Association Review*, 10 (1995), 39-48. On p. 39 Boldridge cites part of the comment on the *Don Quixote* novel that I am quoting more extensively.

[101] See Robert W. Dent, *Proverbial Language in English Drama Exclusive of Shakespeare, 1495-1616. An Index* (Berkeley, California: University of California Press, 1984), p. 735 ("To fight with a windmill"); and Bartlett Jere Whiting, *Early American Proverbs and Proverbial Phrases* (Cambridge, Massachusetts: Harvard University Press, 1977), p. 488 ("To fight [etc.] windmills").

[102] *The Poems of Edmund Waller*, ed. by G. Thorn Dury (New York: Greenwood Press, 1968), p. 106. The poem is entitled "To the Mutable Fair," see pp. 106-108.

[103] Cited from Knowles, "Allusions to *Don Quixote* before 1660," p. 582. I was unable to locate *Loveday's Letters Domestick and Forrein* (London: Nathaniel Brook, 1659).

[104] *The Papers of Alexander Hamilton*, ed. by Harold C. Syrett and Jacob E. Cooke (New York: Columbia University Press, 1961), vol. 2, pp. 22-23. The letter to Susanna Livingston is dated March 18, 1779, see pp. 22-24.

[105] *The Writings of Thomas Jefferson*, ed. by Albert Ellery Bergh (Washington, D.C.: The Thomas Jefferson Memorial Association, 1907), vol. 10, p. 129. The letter is dated August 18, 1799, and is addressed to Edmund Randolph, see pp. 125-129.

[106] *Autobiography, Correspondence, etc., of Lyman Beecher, D.D.*, ed. by Charles Beecher (New York: Harper & Brothers, 1865), vol. 2, p. 85. The letter is dated November 21, 1826, and is addressed to Edward Beecher, see p. 85.

[107] *The Works of William Makepeace Thackeray* (London: Smith, Elder & Co., 1879-1882), vol. 3, p. 803. The reference is from Thackeray's novel *The Newcomes* (1855), end of chapter 67.

[108] Tobias Wells, *A Die in the Country* (Garden City, New York: Doubleday, 1972), p. 151.

[109] Gaylord Larsen, *Dorothy and Agatha* (New York: Dutton, 1990), p. 186.

[110] Albert M. Hyamson, *A Dictionary of English Phrases* (New York: E.P. Dutton, 1922; rpt. Detroit, Michigan: Gale Research Company, 1970), p. 343.

[111] Lurie, *Everyday Sayings*, p. 331. This statement is followed by a half-page summary of the windmill-adventure.

[112] *Oxford English Dictionary*, vol. 10, p. 164. The second edition of the *OED* from 1989 (vol. 20, p. 382) contains the identical statement.

[113] Stevenson, *The Home Book of Proverbs, Maxims, and Famous Phrases*, p. 2516 (no. 8).

[114] Charles Earle Funk, *Heavens to Betsy! And Other Curious Sayings* (New York: Harper & Row, 1955), p. 49. A half-page summary of the windmill-episode is attached.

[115] Sanki Ichikawa et al., *Dictionary of Current English Idioms* (Tokyo: Kenkyusha, 1964), p. 746.

[116] Urdang et al. *Picturesque Expressions: A Thematic Dictionary*, p. 350. A short account of the windmill-chapter follows.

[117] Hendrickson, *The Facts on File Encyclopedia of Word and Phrase Origins*, p. 525. The entry begins with a short summary of the windmill-chapter.

[118] Bartlett Jere Whiting, *Modern Proverbs and Proverbial Sayings* (Cambridge, Massachusetts: Harvard University Press, 1989), p. 688. Whiting offers

no explanation of the phrase, but he lists seven contextualized references from between 1943 and 1972.

[119] Nigel Rees, *Bloomsbury Dictionary of Phrase & Allusion* (London: Bloomsbury, 1991), p. 318.

[120] Elizabeth Knowles, *The Oxford Dictionary of Phrase, Saying, and Quotation* (Oxford: Oxford University Press, 1997), p. 183.

[121] Christine Ammer, *The American Heritage Dictionary of Idioms* (Boston: Houghton Mifflin Company, 1997), p. 663.

[122] George B. Bryan and Wolfgang Mieder, *A Dictionary of Anglo-American Proverbs and Proverbial Phrases Found in Literary Sources of the Nineteenth and Twentieth Centuries* (New York: Peter Lang, 2005), p. 849. The authors give no definition and cite but one reference from 1990: "Perhaps we are only jousting at windmills," in Gaylord Larsen, *Dorothy and Agatha* (New York: Dutton, 1990), p. 246. By placing this text under the lemma "to tilt at (fight) windmills," the two compilers signal that they consider the tilting-variant to be the standard form of the expression, with "to fight windmills" also being quite prevalent.

[123] See Bartlett Jere Whiting, *Early American Proverbs and Proverbial Phrases*, p. 488; and Whiting, *Modern Proverbs and Proverbial Sayings*, p. 688.

[124] *The Complete Works of Edgar Allan Poe*, ed. by James A. Harrison (New York: Thomas Y. Crowell, 1902; rpt. New York: AMS Press, 1965), vol. 10, pp. 182-195 (here p. 194).

[125] Agatha Christie, *Perilous Journeys of Hercule Poirot, including "The Mystery of the Blue Train," "Death on the Nile," and "Murder in Mesopotamia* (New York: Dodd, Mead & Company, 1937), p. 397. The reference is from *Death on the Nile* (chapter xxiv). Cited almost identically in the play version of this detective story; see Agatha Christie, *Murder on the Nile* (London: Samuel French, 1948), p. 54. See also George B. Bryan, *Black Sheep, Red Herrings, and Blue Murder. The Proverbial Agatha Christie* (Bern: Peter Lang, 1993), p. 441.

[126] John Dickson Carr, *The Life of Sir Arthur Conan Doyle* (New York: Harper & Brothers, 1949), p. 157.

[127] E.C.R. Lorac, *Speak Justly of the Dead* (Garden City, New York: Doubleday, 1952), p. 30.

[128] Ursula Curtiss, *Widow's Webb* (New York: Dodd, Mead & Company, 1956), p. 25.

[129] Hammond Innes, *The Doomed Oasis* (New York: Alfred Knopf, 1960), p. 255.

[130] Leonard Woolf, *Growing. An Autobiography of the Years 1904-1911* (New York: Harcourt, Brace & World, 1962), p. 104.

[131] Rhoda Truax, *The Doctors Warren of Boston. First Family of Surgery* (Boston: Houghton Mifflin Company, 1968), p. 255.

[132] Paul Bryers, *The Cat Trapper* (London: André Deutsch, 1978), p. 57.

[133] Morag Joss, *Fearful Symmetry* (New York: Dell, 1999), p. 309. This might be a reference to the ballet music of *Don Quixote* (1869) composed by Ludwig (Léon) Minkus.

[134] Wolfgang Mieder, "'A Man of Fashion Never Has Recourse to Proverbs': Lord Chesterfield's Tilting at Proverbial Windmills," in W. Mieder,

Strategies of Wisdom. Anglo-American and German Proverb Studies (Baltmannsweiler: Schneider Verlag Hohengehren, 2000), pp. 37-68 (here p. 63).

[135] *The New Yorker* (September 27, 1930), p. 19. The artist is Oscar Howard.

[136] This cartoon was found on the "Goofy Faces Caricatures" website. The cartoonist is Paul Taylor, and the date is circa 1990.

[137] Cartoon by the writer Ron Callari and the artist Jack Pittman from 2003. Found on the internet at www.kiddmillennium.com/windmills.htm

[138] Photo-montage from 2004 found in *The Internet Weekly* on the website www.internetweekly.org/images/bush_windmills.jpq

[139] I would like to thank my work-study student Erin Regan for her invaluable help in conducting the analysis of *The New York Times*.

[140] Singer advertisement from 1890/1900, found on the website www.singermemories.com/singer-empire.html

[141] Quoted from Hans Erich Köhler, *Pardon wird nicht gegeben. Karikaturen unserer Zeit* (Hannover: Fackelträger, 1957), no pp. given.

[142] *Der Spiegel*, no. 40 (October 1, 1990), p. 177.

[143] *Die Zeit*, no. 2 (January 4, 2001), p. 1.

[144] *The New Yorker* (November 4, 1944), p. 21. The cartoonist is Alan Dunn.

[145] *Nebelspalter*, no. 39 (September 23, 1980), p. 34.

[146] *The New Yorker* (April 11, 1983), p. 33. The artist is Ed Arno.

[147] *The New Yorker* (August 15, 1988), front cover,

[148] *The New Yorker* (September 9, 1974), p. 33. The artist is Richard Oldden.

[149] *The New Yorker* (November 21, 1977), p. 67. The artist is Donald Reilly.

[150] *Punch* (June 27, 1979), p. 1126.

[151] *The New Yorker* (August 1, 1970), p. 28. The artist is Ed Fisher.

[152] *Punch* (August 26, 1970), p. 306.

[153] *Punch* (April 26, 1972), p. 573.

[154] Cartoon by Les Barton from circa 1990. Found on the website of "Goofy Faces Caricatures."

[155] *The New Yorker* (October 11, 1993), p. 89.

[156] *The New Yorker* (August 26, 1993), p. 61.

[157] *Saturday Review* (April 22, 1977), p. 30.

[158] *The New Yorker* (August 24, 1998), p. 65.

Appendix

When I wrote this monograph during the summer of 2005 to help celebrate the 400th birthday of Miguel de Cervantes Saavedra's novel *Don Quixote* (1605) at the twelfth annual Hispanic Forum on October 20, 2005, at the University of Vermont, I included thirty-eight illustrations in the shortened version of my lecture. While they are now also part of this more detailed publication, I actually knew all along that my international proverb archives contain seventeen additional references that might be of interest even though I did not need them for my lecture/monograph a year ago. In fact, a few of them do not deal with the windmill-episode but instead with some other aspects of the novel. However, now that my study is appearing in print, I have decided to include these invaluable sources in this section by maintaining the consecutive count of the illustrations.

The majority of the caricatures and cartoons depicted here come from the two German satirical magazines *Simplicissimus* and *Kladderadatsch*. They deal for the most part with political and social issues of the first half of the twentieth century. While the meaning of some of them is not absolutely clear today, the illustrations of Don Quixote and Sancho Panza in front of the windmills speak more or less for themselves. I have, however, translated the German titles, captions and/or verses and where necessary and possible, I have also provided short explanatory comments.

The additional Anglo-American references come primarily from *Punch* and *The New Yorker*. They are not so much political caricatures but rather cartoons that include a social message or are meant to be humorous allusions to the novel and its popularity. This is certainly obvious from the last cartoon with Don Quixote explaining in the caption "I'm quixotic. He's panzaesque" (1980), a most telling indication that Don Quixote and Sancho Panza have become types or motifs in themselves, just as Don Quixote's fight against the windmills has reached a proverbial status in many languages and cultures.

The additional iconographic references in this appendix are thus to be understood as further proofs that the image of tilting at windmills belongs to modern cultural literacy as both a visual and verbal sign of the human condition.

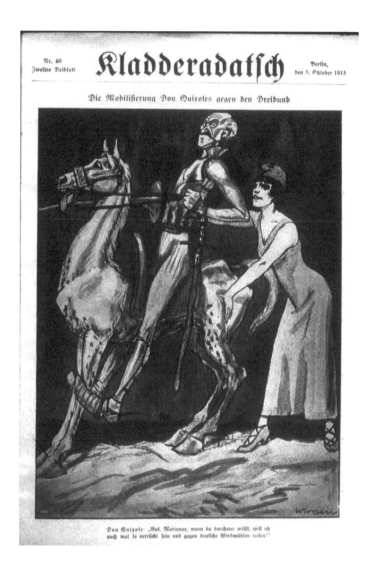

Figure 39: *Kladderadatsch*, no. 40 (October 5, 1913), p. 4.
Artist: W. Krain

The Mobilization of Don Quixote against the Triple Alliance.
[alliance among Germany, Austria-Hungary, and Italy against France
and Russia]
Don Quixote: "Okay, Marianne [i.e., France], if you absolutely insist,
I will for once be crazy enough to ride against German windmills!"

Figure 40: *Simplicissimus*, 21, no. 3 (April 18, 1916), p. 44.
Artist: Olaf Gulbransson

Don Quixote-Grey and Vittorio-Sancho Panza.
[Sir Edward Grey, British Foreign Secretary, made various promises to the Italians (including King Vittorio Emanuele and minister Vittorio Orlando) before they left the Triple Alliance during World War I]
"By God, Knight of the Sad Countenance, sometimes I have the thought that everything that you say about winning kingdoms and empires and giving islands as presents and handing out favors and splendors is nothing but empty talk and lies and dumplings of air or castles in the air."

101

München, 4. Juni 1923   Preis 1000 Mark   28. Jahrgang Nr. 10

SIMPLICISSIMUS

Begründet von Albert Langen und Th. Th. Heine

Der französische Ritter von der traurigen Gestalt

„Bekommst du nicht das Mehl, so machst du wenigstens die Windmühle kaputt."

Figure 41: *Simplicissimus*, 28, no. 10 (June 4, 1923), p. 117.
Artist: Wilhelm Schulz

The French Knight of the Sad Countenance.
"Even if you don't get the flour, you will at least destroy the windmill."

102

Figure 42: Juan Givanel Mas y Gaziel, *Historia Gráfica de Cervantes y del Quijote.* Madrid: Editorial Plus-Ultra, 1946, p. 507 (ill. 289).

Ilustration from a Japanese children's book about Don Quixote from 1925.

Figure 43: *Kladderadatsch*, no. 15 (April 11, 1926), title page.
Artist: Johnson

Going Dry!
The New Don Quixote Intoxicated by Anti-Alcoholism!
Poor fool, why don't you just give up!
If only you had drunk the good wine;
You would not have sunk so low,
For now you are tipsy *without* wine!

Figure 44: *Simplicissimus*, 33, no. 50 (March 11, 1929), p. 645.
Artist: Olaf Gulbransson

In the Country of Don Quixote
When the servant mounts the high horse,
Only the donkey is left for the master.

105

Figure 45: *Kladderadatsch*, no. 41 (October 1929), title page. Artist: Werner Sahmann

Doña Quixote [as the liberal press]
Ha, does the good aunt jump
High on her Rocinante
And fight with anger and fear
Against a tiger?? No – against a mouse!

„Stell' dir vor, Sancho Pansa, das gute Spanien hat mich einen Narren gescholten, weil ich vor Jahrhunderten gegen böse Fabelwesen kämpfte — und nun sind sie rote Wirklichkeit!"

Figure 46: *Simplicissimus*, 41, no. 36 (November 29, 1936), p. 467.
Artist: Wilhelm Schulz

Don Quixote's Justification
"Imagine, Sancho Panza, good old Spain called me a fool because I fought against wicked apparitions centuries ago – and now they are red [i.e., communist] reality!"

107

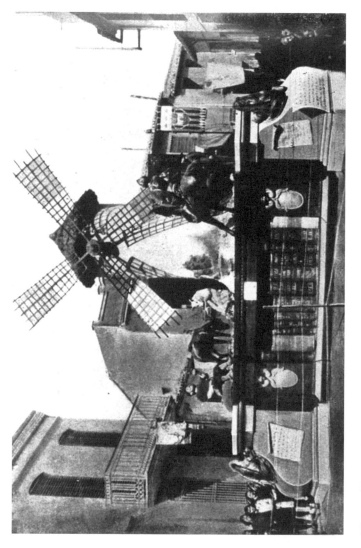

Figure 47: Juan Givanel Mas y Gaziel, *Historia Gráfica de Cervantes y del Quijote*. Madrid: Editorial Plus-Ultra, 1946, p. 352 (ill. 192).

A photograph of the windmill adventure in a street display from 1945 at Burriana, Spain.

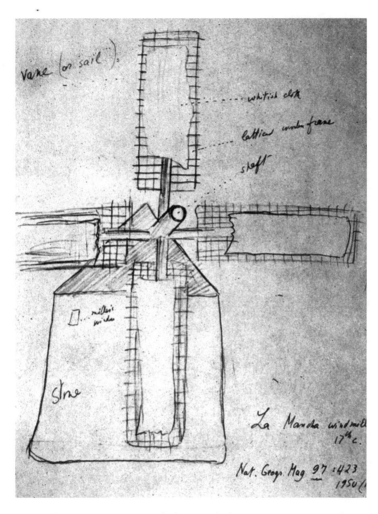

Figure 48: Fredson Bowers, *Vladimir Nabokov. Lectures on Don Quixote.*
New York: Harcourt, Brace, Jovanovich, 1983, p. ii.

Drawing by Vladimir Nabokov for his lectures on *Don Quixote* that he delivered as guest professor at Harvard University during the spring semes-
ter of 1952.

Figure 49: *Simplicissimus*, no. 10 (March 9, 1963), p. 153.
Artist: Manfred Oesterle

In Honor of the Magnificent Dulcinea Europe
"Don't run away, you cowardly and base creatures! It's but one knight
who is confronting you!"

Figure 50: *The New Yorker* (September 24, 1966), p. 57. Artist: Saul Steinberg [a female Doña Quixote - a possible reference to women's lib?]

Figure 51: Song and text from 1977; cited in *Pan*, no. 5 (April 27, 1990), p. 78. Artist: Boskamp

Those who sit on the high horse
and spill their own blood
those I accept without complaint
even if things are often not clear
they deal with the danger themselves.

But to let others from safety
rush against windmills
that I find nasty –
do I alone think that?
The wise ones often ride on the donkey.

Figure 52: *Tageszeitung* (September 18, 1990), p. 5 Artist: Nico

"Don't we have any agreement yet to throw Sancho Panza from the saddle?"
[dealing with monetary and banking issues]

113

CROSSED PATHS

Toulouse-Lautrec Meets Don Quixote

Figure 53: *The New Yorker* (April 8, 1991), p. 39. Artist: Ronald Searle

[reference to Henri de Toulouse-Lautrec's (1864-1901) painting "At the Moulin Rouge" (1892), with Don Quixote saving his Dulcinea from the painter]

„Ich bin zwar ein Kämpfer, aber kein Don Quijote"

Figure 54: *Die Zeit*, no. 23 (June 10, 1994), p. 11.

"To be sure, I am a fighter, but I am no Don Quixote."
[the accompanying article by Ralf Rumpel deals with the new management idea where managers take on their high level jobs for only an agreed upon time period]

"No, **I'm** quixotic. **He's** panzaesque."

Figure 55: *Punch* (October 29, 1980), p. 766. Artist: F. Folkes

[allusion to the character traits of both Don Quixote and Sancho Panza that have become stereotypically proverbial as a sign of cultural literacy regarding Cervantes' novel *Don Quixote*]

Supplement Series
of
Proverbium
Yearbook of International Proverb Scholarship

Volume 1:
Knappert, Jan. *Swahili Proverbs*. Burlington, Vermont: The University of Vermont, 1997. 156 pp. [out of print]

Volume 2:
Mieder, Wolfgang. *"A House Divided": From Biblical Proverb to Lincoln and Beyond*. Burlington, Vermont: The University of Vermont, 1998. 163 pp. [out of print]

Volume 3:
McKenna, Kevin J. (ed.). *Proverbs in Russian Literature: From Catherine the Great to Alexander Solzhenitsyn*. Burlington, Vermont: The University of Vermont, 1998. 113 pp.

Volume 4:
Mieder, Wolfgang, and Anna Tóthné Litovkina. *Twisted Wisdom: Modern Anti-Proverbs*. Burlington, Vermont: The University of Vermont, 1999. 254 pp. [out of print]

Volume 5:
Trokhimenko, Olga V. *"Wie ein Elefant im Porzellanladen": Zur Weltgeschichte einer Redensart*. Burlington, Vermont: The University of Vermont, 1999. 186 pp.

Volume 6:
Mieder, Wolfgang (ed.). *Sprichwörter bringen es an den Tag: Parömiologische Studien zu Lessing, Brecht, Zuckmayer, Kaschnitz, Kaléko und Eschker*. Burlington, Vermont: The University of Vermont, 2000. 269 pp. [out of print]

Volume 7:
Mieder, Wolfgang, and Deborah Holmes. *"Children and Proverbs Speak the Truth": Teaching Proverbial Wisdom to Fourth*

Graders. Burlington, Vermont: The University of Vermont, 2000. 240 pp.

Volume 8:
Pritchard, Ilka Maria. *"Des Volkes Stimme ist auch eine Stimme": Zur Sprichwörtlichkeit in Carl Zuckmayers Dramen "Der fröhliche Weinberg", "Der Hauptmann von Köpenick" und "Des Teufels General".* Burlington, Vermont: The University of Vermont, 2001. 171 pp. [ISBN 0-9710223-0-5]

Volume 9:
Mieder, Wolfgang (ed.). *"Geht einmal euren Phrasen nach": Sprachkritische Lyrik und Kurzprosa zur deutschen Vergangenheit.* Burlington, Vermont: The University of Vermont, 2001. 219 pp. [ISBN 0-9710223-1-3]

Volume 10:
Mieder, Wolfgang (ed.). *"In der Kürze liegt die Würze": Sprichwörtliches und Spruchhaftes als Basis für Aphoristisches.* Burlington, Vermont: The University of Vermont, 2002. 159 pp. [ISBN 0-9710223-3-X]

Volume 11:
Kelly, Walter K. *A Collection of the Proverbs of All Nations* [1859], reprint ed. by Wolfgang Mieder. Burlington, Vermont: The University of Vermont, 2002. 245 pp. [ISBN 0-9710223- 5-6]

Volume 12:
Williams, Fionnuala Carson. *Wellerisms in Ireland: Towards a Corpus from Oral and Literary Sources.* Burlington, Vermont: The University of Vermont, 2002. 321 pp. [ISBN 0-9710223-2- 1]

Volume 13:
Trench, Richard Chenevix. *Proverbs and Their Lessons* [1853, 1905], reprint ed. by Wolfgang Mieder. Burlington, Vermont: The University of Vermont, 2003. 185 pp. [ISBN 0-9710223-4- 8]

Volume 14:
Hose, Susanne, and Wolfgang Mieder (eds.). *Sorbian Proverbs.*
Serbske přisłowa. Burlington, Vermont: The University of Vermont, 2004. 149 pp. [ISBN 0-9710223-6-4]

Volume 15:
Mieder, Wolfgang (ed.) "Liebe macht blind": Sprichwörtliche
Lyrik und Kurzprosa zum Thema der Liebe. Burlington, Vermont: The University of Vermont, 2004. 247 pp.
[ISBN 0-9710223-7-2]

Volume 16:
Mieder, Wolfgang (ed.). *"The Netherlandish Proverbs": An International Proverb Symposium on the Pieter Brueg(h)els.* Burlington, Vermont: The University of Vermont, 2004. 243 pp.
[ISBN 0-9710223-8-0]

Volume 17:
Cantera Ortiz de Urbina, Jesús, Julia Sevilla Muñoz, and Manuel Sevilla Muñoz. *Refranes, otras paremias y fraseologismos en "Don Quijote de la Mancha".* Burlington, Vermont: The University of Vermont, 2005. 200 pp. [ISBN 0-9710223-9-9]

Volume 18:
Mieder, Wolfgang, and Janet Sobieski (eds.). *"So Many Heads, So Many Wits": An Anthology of English Proverb Poetry.* Burlington, Vermont: The University of Vermont, 2005. 278 pp.
[ISBN 0-9770731-0-6]

Volume 19:
Mieder, Wolfgang (ed.). *"Best of All Possible Friends": Three Decades of Correspondence Between the Folklorists Alan Dundes and Wolfgang Mieder.* Burlington, Vermont: The University of Vermont, 2006. 313 pp. [ISBN 0-9770731-1-4]

Volume 20:
Röhrich, Lutz. *Gebärde-Metapher-Parodie. Studien zur Sprache und Volksdichtung* [1967], reprint ed. by Wolfgang Mieder. Burlington, Vermont: The University of Vermont, 2006. 246 pp.
[ISBN 0-9770731-2-2]